Eggs

BLOOMSBURY KITCHEN LIBRARY

Eggs

Bloomsbury Books
London

This edition published 1994 by Bloomsbury Books,
an imprint of The Godfrey Cave Group,
42 Bloomsbury Street, London, WC1B 3QJ.

ISBN 1 85471 522 4

Printed and bound in Great Britain.

Contents

Pastry Cream

Makes about 30 cl (½ pint)

Working time: about 25 minutes

Total time: about 1 hour and 50 minutes (includes chilling)

2	egg yolks	**2**	**30 cl**	skimmed milk	**½ pint**
30 g	caster sugar	**1 oz**	**1 tsp**	pure vanilla extract	**1 tsp**
30 g	plain flour, sifted	**1 oz**	**2 tbsp**	thick Greek yogurt	**2 tbsp**
15 g	cornflour, sifted	**½ oz**	**1**	egg white	**1**

Put the egg yolks and half the caster sugar into a bowl. Whisk them together until thick, then carefully fold in the flour and cornflour.

Heat the milk and vanilla extract together in a saucepan until hot but not boiling. Gradually whisk the hot milk into the egg mixture, then strain the mixture through a nylon sieve back into the pan. Stir the custard over a low heat until it comes to the boil, then simmer it, stirring continuously, for 5 to 6 minutes, or until no taste of raw flour remains, do not let the custard burn during this time. Remove the pan from the heat, spoon the custard into a bowl and cover the surface closely with plastic film to prevent a skin forming. Allow to cool for about 10 minutes, then refrigerate until almost, but not quite, cold – 15 to 20 minutes.

Whisk the custard until it is smooth, then whisk in the yogurt. In another bowl, whisk the egg white until stiff, then whisk in the remaining sugar until shiny. Gradually fold the egg white into the custard. Cover the bowl with plastic film and chill the pastry cream for at least 1 hour.

Orange-flavoured pastry cream. Add the finely grated rind of one orange to the milk. Whisk 1 tablespoon of Grand Marnier into the cooled custard before adding the whisked egg white.

Chocolate-flavoured pastry cream. Melt 30 g (1 oz) of plain chocolate in the hot milk in the saucepan.

Liqueur-flavoured pastry cream. Whisk 1 tablespoon of rum, brandy or liqueur such as Cointreau, kirsch or Tia Maria into the cooled custard before adding the whisked egg white.

Genoese Sponge

**Makes
one 30 by
20 cm
(12 by 8 inch)
sponge**

**Working
time: about
20 minutes**

**Total time:
about
1 hour**

3	eggs	3
1	egg white	1
90 g	caster sugar	3 oz

125 g	plain flour	4 oz
30 g	unsalted butter, melted and cooled slightly	1 oz

Preheat the oven to 180°C (350°F or Mark 4). Butter a 30 by 20 by 4 cm (12 by 8 by 1½ inch) rectangular tin and line the base with non-stick parchmont paper.

Put the eggs, egg white and caster sugar into a mixing bowl. Set the bowl over a saucepan of hot, but not boiling, water on a low heat. Using an electric hand-held mixer, whisk the eggs and sugar together until thick and very pale. Remove the bowl from the saucepan and continue whisking until the mixture is cool and falls from the whisk in a ribbon trail. Sift the flour very lightly over the surface of the egg and sugar mixture, then fold it in gently using a large metal spoon. Gradually fold in the melted butter.

Pour the sponge batter into the prepared tin and spread it evenly. Bake it for 25 to 30 minutes, until well risen, springy to the touch and very slightly shrunk from the sides of the tin. Carefully unmould the sponge on to a wire rack. Loosen the parchment paper but do not remove it. Place another wire rack on top of the paper, then invert both racks together so that the sponge is right side up on top of the paper. Remove the top rack and allow the sponge to cool.

Editor's Note: Individual recipes do not always use the full quantity of sponge prepared here. Leftover sponge may be stored in an airtight tin for several days.

Overnight French Toast

Serves 6

Working time: about 30 minutes

Total time: about 8 hours and 30 minutes (includes chilling)

Calories 300

Protein 12g

Cholesterol 100mg

Total fat 4g

Saturated fat 2g

Sodium 530mg

1	loaf (about 500 g/1 lb) French bread, the ends trimmed	1	
2	eggs, plus 2 egg whites	2	
6 tbsp	caster sugar	6 tbsp	
2	lemons, grated rind only	2	

¼ tsp	salt	¼ tsp
½ litre	semi-skimmed milk	16 fl oz
2 tbsp	light or dark rum, or 1 tsp pure vanilla extract	2 tbsp
	freshly grated nutmeg	

Cut the bread into 12 slices about 2 cm (¾ inch) thick. In a large, shallow dish, whisk together the eggs, egg whites, sugar, lemon rind and salt, then whisk in the milk and the rum or vanilla extract.

Dip the bread slices into the egg-and-milk mixture, turning them once or twice until they are thoroughly soaked with the liquid. Transfer the slices to a large plate as you work. Dribble any liquid remaining in the dish over the slices, then sprinkle some nutmeg over them. Cover the slices with plastic film and refrigerate them overnight.

Preheat the oven to 200°C (400°F or Mark 6). Heat a large griddle or frying pan over medium heat until a few drops of cold water dance when sprinkled on the surface. Put as many prepared bread slices as will fit on the griddle or pan and cook them until the undersides are golden – about 3 minutes. Turn the slices and cook them until the second sides are lightly browned – 2 to 3 minutes more. Transfer the slices to a baking sheet. Brown the remaining slices and transfer them to the baking sheet.

Place the baking sheet in the oven and bake the French toast until it is cooked through and has puffed up – about 10 minutes. Serve it hot with blueberry syrup or another topping of your choice.

Editor's Note: Allowing the soaked bread slices to rest overnight yields soft and creamy centres.

Tropical Puffed Pancake

Serves 4

Working time: about 30 minutes

Total time: about 45 minutes

Calories 350

Protein 9g

Cholesterol 140mg

Total fat 8g

Saturated fat 2g

Sodium 265mg

3 tbsp	caster sugar	3 tbsp
¼ tsp	ground cinnamon	¼ tsp
35 g	plain flour	1¼ oz
30 g	wholemeal flour	1 oz
½ tsp	baking powder	½ tsp
¼ tsp	salt	¼ tsp
2	eggs, separated, plus 1 egg white	2
1 tbsp	light or dark rum	1 tbsp
1 tbsp	safflower oil	1 tbsp
1	lemon, grated rind only	1
17.5 cl	semi-skimmed milk	6 fl oz

2	bananas, sliced diagonally into 5 mm (¼ inch) thick ovals	2
	Rum-Pineapple Topping	
300 g	fresh pineapple flesh, coarsely chopped, or canned unsweetened pineapple chunks, drained and coarsely chopped	10 oz
2 tbsp	dark brown sugar	2 tbsp
2 tbsp	raisins	2 tbsp
1	lemon, juice only	1
2 tbsp	light or dark rum	2 tbsp

Put the pineapple into a saucepan and stir in the brown sugar, raisins and lemon juice. Bring to the boil, then simmer for 5 minutes. Remove from the heat and stir in the rum. Keep the topping warm.

In a small bowl, mix 2 tablespoons of the sugar with the cinnamon; set aside. Preheat the oven to 220°C (425°F or Mark 7).

Sift the flours, baking powder, salt and remaining sugar into a bowl. In a bowl, whisk the egg yolks with the rum and oil; stir in lemon rind and milk. Whisk the flour mixture into the milk mixture to make a smooth, thin batter.

Beat the egg whites until they form soft peaks. Stir half into the batter and then fold in the remainder.

Heat a 30 cm (12 inch) shallow casserole over medium heat. Ladle the batter into the casserole. Cook the pancake for 2 minutes; top it with the sliced bananas and sprinkle it with the cinnamon sugar. Put into the oven until it puffs up and is golden-brown – 10 to 12 minutes. Slide the puffed pancake out of the casserole on to a warmed serving plate. Serve it immediately with the rum-pineapple topping.

Cornmeal Buttermilk Pancakes

Serves 6

Working (and total) time: about 20 minutes

Calories 285
Protein 8g
Cholesterol 95mg
Total fat 7g
Saturated fat 1g
Sodium 245mg

175 g	plain flour	6 oz	125 g	cornmeal	4 oz
3 tbsp	caster sugar	3 tbsp	2	eggs	2
½ tsp.	bicarbonate of soda	½ tsp	35 cl	buttermilk	12 fl oz
¼ tsp	salt	¼ tsp	2 tbsp	safflower oil	2 tbsp

Sift the flour, sugar, bicarbonate of soda and salt into a bowl; stir in the cornmeal. In another bowl whisk together the eggs, buttermilk and oil.

Pour the buttermilk mixture into the dry ingredients and whisk them quickly together until they are just blended; do not overmix.

Heat a large griddle or frying pan over medium heat until a few drops of cold water dance when sprinkled on the surface. Drop 2 tablespoons of the batter on to the hot griddle or pan, and use the back of the spoon to spread the batter into a round. Fill the pan with pancakes; cook them until the tops are covered with bubbles and the undersides are golden – 1 to 2 minutes. Flip the pancakes over and cook them until the second sides are lightly browned – about 1 minute more. Transfer the pancakes to a platter and keep them warm while you cook the remaining batter.

Serve the pancakes immediately, accompanied by a topping of your choice.

Rye Griddle Cakes

Serves 8

Working time: about 30 minutes

Calories 155

Protein 10g

Cholesterol 80mg

Total fat 3g

Saturated fat 1g

Sodium 315mg

2	eggs, plus 2 egg whites	2
15 cl	semi-skimmed milk	¼ pint
2	large spring onions, trimmed and finely chopped	2
¼ tsp	salt	¼ tsp
	freshly ground black pepper	
250 g	fresh dark rye breadcrumbs (made from about ½ loaf of dark rye bread)	8 oz

Accompaniments

175 g	yogurt cheese	6 oz
1 tbsp	red lumpfish caviare	1 tbsp
1	spring onion, sliced diagonally	1
1	lemon, thinly sliced (optional)	1

Whisk together the eggs, egg whites, milk, finely chopped spring onions, salt and a generous grinding of pepper in a bowl. Stir in the breadcrumbs to make a smooth mixture.

Heat a large griddle or frying pan over medium heat until a few drops of water dance when sprinkled on the surface. Drop the batter 1 generous tablespoon at a time on to the griddle or pan, and use the back of the spoon to spread the batter into ovals. Cook the griddle cakes until they are covered with bubbles – 1 to 3 minutes. Turn each cake and cook the second side for 1 minute more. Transfer the cakes to a platter and keep them warm while you cook the remaining batter.

Accompany each serving with a dollop of yogurt cheese topped with some caviare and sliced spring onion; if you wish, garnish with a slice of lemon.

Editor's Note: Plain low-fat yogurt may be substituted for the yogurt cheese.

Puffy Fruit Omelette

2	eggs, separated, plus 2 egg whites	**2**
2 tbsp	plain flour	**2 tbsp**
½ tsp	baking powder	**½ tsp**
⅛ tsp	salt	**⅛ tsp**
12.5 cl	semi-skimmed milk	**4 fl oz**
15 g	caster sugar	**½ oz**
1	red eating apple, quartered, cored and cut into 1 cm (½ inch) pieces	**1**
1 tsp	safflower oil	**1 tsp**
1	pear, quartered, cored and cut into 1 cm (½ inch) pieces	**1**
1 tsp	fresh lemon juice	**1 tsp**
¼ tsp	ground cinnamon	**¼ tsp**
2 tbsp	raspberry jam	**2 tbsp**
2 tbsp	unsweetened apple juice	**2 tbsp**

Preheat the oven to 230°C (450°F or Mark 8). In a bowl, whisk together the egg yolks, flour, baking powder, salt and 3 tablespoons of the milk until the mixture is well blended – 5 to 7 minutes. Whisk in the remaining milk.

In another bowl, beat the egg whites with 3 teaspoons of the sugar until they form soft peaks. Stir half into the yolk mixture and then fold in the remainder until the mixture is just blended; do not overmix. Set the egg mixture aside.

Heat the oil in a large, shallow proof casserole over medium-high heat. Add the apple and the pear, the remaining sugar, the lemon juice and the cinnamon and cook the fruit, stirring frequently, until it is tender – about 5 minutes. Remove the casserole from the heat and pour the egg mixture over the fruit; smooth the top of the mixture. Place the casserole in the oven and bake the omelette until the top is golden-brown – 10 to 15 minutes.

While the omelette is baking, mix together the raspberry jam and the unsweetened apple juice in a small dish. When the omelette is ready, dribble this syrup over it, slice it into quarters and serve immediately.

Frittata with Mozzarella Cheese

Serves 4
as a
main dish

Working
(and total)
time: about
35 minutes

Calories
170
Protein
11g
Cholesterol
85mg
Total fat
11g
Saturated fat
4g
Sodium
320mg

1	egg, plus 2 egg whites	1
¼ tsp	salt	¼ tsp
	freshly ground black pepper	
4 tbsp	low-fat ricotta cheese	4 tbsp
1½ tbsp	virgin olive oil	1½ tbsp
90 g	mushrooms, wiped clean and sliced	3 oz
2	garlic cloves, finely chopped	2
1½ tsp	fresh thyme, or ½ tsp dried thyme	1½ tsp
3	spring onions, trimmed and cut into 1 cm (½ inch) pieces, white and green parts separated	3
250 g	courgettes, cut into bâtons	8 oz
1	sweet red pepper, seeded, deribbed and sliced into thin strips	1
1½ tsp	fresh lemon juice	1½ tsp
2 tbsp	freshly grated Parmesan cheese	2 tbsp
60 g	low-fat mozzarella, cut into thin strips	2 oz

In a bowl, whisk together the egg, egg whites, ⅛ teaspoon of the salt, some pepper, the ricotta and ½ tablespoon of the oil, and set the mixture aside.

Preheat grill. Heat the remaining tablespoon of oil in a large, shallow, non-stick fireproof casserole over high heat. Add the mushrooms, garlic, thyme, the white parts of the spring onions and some pepper. Cook the vegetable mixture until the mushrooms are lightly browned – 2 to 3 minutes. Add the courgettes, red pepper, the remaining salt and the lemon juice, and cook the mixture, stirring frequently, until the

vegetables are tender and all of the liquid has evaporated – about 5 minutes.

Remove the casserole from the heat and stir the spring onion greens and the Parmesan cheese into the vegetable mixture. Press the vegetables into an even layer and pour in the egg mixture. Cook the frittata over medium heat for 1 minute. Sprinkle the mozzarella evenly over the frittata and place the casserole under the preheated grill. Grill until the cheese begins to brown – 2 to 3 minutes. Slide the frittata on to a warm serving plate. Serve immediately.

Omelettes Stuffed with Seafood and Bean Sprouts

Serves 4

Working
(and total)
time: about
35 minutes

Calories
160

Protein
13g

Cholesterol
105mg

Total fat
8g

Saturated fat
1g

Sodium
85mg

3 tbsp	rice vinegar	**3 tbsp**
1 tbsp	caster sugar	**1 tbsp**
1 tbsp	fresh lemon juice	**1 tbsp**
250 g	bean sprouts	**8 oz**
125 g	French beans, trimmed and cut diagonally into thin slices	**4 oz**
1 tbsp	plus 2 tsp safflower oil	**1 tbsp**
1 tsp	curry powder	**1 tsp**
	freshly ground black pepper	
60 g	cooked peeled prawns, chopped	**2 oz**
125 g	sole or plaice fillets, cut into strips	**4 oz**
2	spring onions, thinly sliced	**2**
1	egg, plus 3 egg whites	**1**

Mix the vinegar, 2 teaspoons of the sugar and the lemon juice in a small bowl.

Blanch the bean sprouts and the beans in boiling water for 30 seconds. Drain and rinse the vegetables. Set them aside in a sieve.

Heat 1 teaspoon of oil in a large, non-stick frying pan over medium-high heat. Add the vegetables and cook, stirring frequently, for 2 minutes. Add half the curry powder, half the vinegar mixture and a generous grinding of pepper. Stir and cook until the liquid has evaporated – about 2 minutes. Transfer to a bowl.

Return the pan to the heat and pour in 1 tablespoon of the oil. Add the prawns, fish, and spring onions and cook, stirring frequently, for 1 minute. Add the remaining vinegar mixture, then stir in the vegetable mixture. Cook, stirring frequently, until the liquid has evaporated – 2 to 4 minutes. Set the seafood and vegetables aside.

Whisk the egg, egg whites, the remaining curry powder, sugar, oil and some pepper. With a paper towel, clean the pan the seafood and vegetables were cooked in and heat over medium heat. Pour 4 tablespoons of the egg mixture into the hot pan and swirl it around. Cook the omelette for 30 seconds, turn, and cook for 10 seconds. Transfer to a warm plate, fill with ¼ of filling and fold in half. Repeat process with remaining omelettes and serve immediately.

Spaghetti Omelette

Serves 8
as a
side dish

Working
(and total)
time: about
1 hour

Calories
120

Protein
7g

Cholesterol
6mg

Total fat
3g

Saturated fat
1g

Sodium
260mg

800 g	canned whole tomatoes, with their juice	1¾ lb		1 tbsp	chopped parsley	1 tbsp
125 g	spaghetti, spaghettini or linguine	4 oz		3 tbsp	freshly grated Parmesan cheese	3 tbsp
½ tsp	salt	½ tsp			freshly ground black pepper	
2	egg whites	2		1 tsp	grated lemon rind	1 tsp
12.5 cl	semi-skimmed milk	4 fl oz		2 tsp	virgin olive oil	2 tsp
				60 g	low-fat mozzarella cheese, grated	2 oz

Put the tomatoes into a heavy-bottomed pan. Simmer the tomatoes, stirring occasionally, until the mixture thickens – 20 to 30 minutes.

Boil 2 litres (3½ pints) of water with 1 teaspoon of salt. Add the pasta. Cook the pasta until it is *al dente* – about 8 minutes. Drain the pasta, and rinse it thoroughly.

In a large bowl, beat together the egg whites, milk, parsley, Parmesan, a generous grinding of pepper, the salt and the lemon rind. Toss the pasta with the egg white mixture.

Heat a 22 cm (9 inch) non-stick frying pan over medium-high heat. Add the oil, let it heat for 10 seconds and then evenly coat the bottom with the oil. Put half of the pasta mixture into the pan; smooth the mixture into an even layer.

Reduce the heat to medium. Sprinkle the mozzarella over the pasta mixture and cover it with the remaining mixture. Let the omelette cook slowly until it is firm and the bottom and sides are browned – about 8 minutes.

Slide the omelette on to a plate. Invert the pan over the plate and turn both over together. Cook the second side of the omelette until it, too, is browned – approximately 8 minutes longer.

While omelette is cooking, make the sauce: work the cooked tomatoes through a sieve, discard the seeds and warm.

Slide the omelette on to a warmed serving platter. Serve immediately, passing the sauce separately.

16

Broccoli and Ricotta Pie

Serves 6
as a
main dish

Working
time: about
1 hour

Total time:
about
2 hours

Calories
325

Protein
17g

Cholesterol
65mg

Total fat
8g

Saturated fat
3g

Sodium
285mg

1 tbsp	easy-blend dried yeast	1 tbsp	17.5 cl	semi-skimmed milk		6 fl oz
375 g	strong plain flour	13 oz		freshly ground black pepper		
¼ tsp	salt	¼ tsp	⅛ tsp	grated nutmeg		⅛ tsp
1 tbsp	virgin olive oil	1 tbsp	30 g	mild back bacon, finely chopped		1 oz
250 g	onion, chopped	8 oz	1 tbsp	cornmeal		1 tbsp
½ tsp	caraway seeds, or 2 tsp dried dill	½ tsp	350 g	broccoli florets, blanched in		12 oz
1	egg, plus 2 egg whites	1		boiling water for 1 minute, drained		
175 g	low-fat ricotta cheese	6 oz	2 tbsp	freshly grated Parmesan cheese		2 tbsp

In a bowl, mix the yeast with 140 g (5 oz) of the flour and ⅛ teaspoon of the salt. Pour 17.5 cl (6 fl oz) of warm water into the flour mixture and stir the dough vigorously. Stir in 1 teaspoon of the oil and another 140 g (5 oz) of the flour. Knead on a floured surface. If it seems too sticky, gradually add remaining flour; if too dry, add water, 1 teaspoon at a time. Knead until smooth and elastic – about 10 minutes. Transfer to an oiled bowl and cover the bowl with a damp towel. Let the dough rise in a warm draught-free place until it has doubled in volume – about 30 minutes.

Heat the remaining oil in a heavy frying pan over medium-high heat. Add the onion and the caraway seeds or dill and cook, stirring frequently, for about

10 minutes. Remove the pan from the heat.

Whisk the egg and egg whites in a large bowl. Whisk in the ricotta, milk, remaining salt, some black pepper, nutmeg and bacon. Stir in half the onion mixture.

Preheat the oven to 200°C (400°F or Mark 6). Knock back the dough and knead the remaining onion mixture into it.

Sprinkle a 20 cm (8 inch) shallow fireproof casserole with the cornmeal. Place dough in casserole and work towards the edge to form a rim.

Partially bake the dough 10 minutes. Pour egg mixture into centre; add broccoli florets and sprinkle with Parmesan cheese. Bake for 35 – 40 minutes, until set.

Layered Bread, Tomato and Courgette Casserole

Serves 8
as a
main dish

Working
time: about
1 hour

Total time:
about
1 hour
30 minutes

Calories
200

Protein
12g

Cholesterol
80mg

Total fat
5g

Saturated fat
2g

Sodium
375mg

2	eggs, plus 2 egg whites	2		¼ tsp	salt	¼ tsp
¼ litre	semi-skimmed milk	8 fl oz			freshly ground black pepper	
250 g	small courgettes, cut into 5 mm (¼ inch) thick rounds	8 oz		4 tbsp	chopped parsley	4 tbsp
1	onion, chopped	1		2 tbsp	chopped fresh basil, or 2 tsp dried basil	2 tbsp
4	ripe tomatoes, skinned, seeded and chopped, or 400 g (14 oz) canned whole tomatoes, drained and chopped	4		8	slices French bread, cut into 1 cm (½ inch) cubes	8
				125 g	low-fat mozzarella cheese, grated	4 oz

Whisk the eggs, egg whites, milk, salt and some pepper together in a bowl and set it aside. Preheat the oven to 180°C (350°F or Mark 5).

Put the courgettes and onion into a non-stick frying pan over low heat and cook them, covered, until they are soft – about 4 minutes. Add the tomatoes and increase the heat to high. Cook the vegetables, stirring continuously, until most of the liquid has evaporated – about 5 minutes. Remove the pan from the heat and stir in the parsley and basil.

Spoon half of the vegetable mixture into a

20 cm (8 by 12 inch) baking dish; add half of the bread cubes and sprinkle half of the cheese over the bread. Repeat the process with the remaining vegetable mixture, bread and cheese, then pour the egg mixture over all.

Bake the casserole until the egg mixture has set – about 20 minutes. Increase the oven temperature to 230°C (450°F or Mark 8) and continue baking the casserole until it is lightly browned – about 5 minutes more. Cut the casserole into eight squares and serve it hot.

Tomato Soufflé

Serves 4
as a
main dish
or 8 as
a side dish

Working
time: about
40 minutes

Total time:
about
1 hour and
40 minutes

Calories
190

Protein
3g

Cholesterol
70mg

Total fat
5g

Saturated fat
1g

Sodium
220mg

350 g	large new potatoes, peeled and quartered	**12 oz**
400 g	canned whole tomatoes, seeded, the juice reserved	**14 oz**
1 tsp	sugar	**1 tsp**
1	onion, chopped	**1**
1½ tbsp	chopped fresh ginger root	**1½ tbsp**

2	garlic cloves, finely chopped	**2**
1	large ripe tomato, skinned	**1**
2 tbsp	plain flour	**2 tbsp**
1	egg, separated, plus 4 egg whites	**1**
¼ tsp	salt	**¼ tsp**
	freshly ground black pepper	
1 tbsp	virgin olive oil	**1 tbsp**

Boil the potatoes until they are tender – 15 to 20 minutes. Drain the potatoes and return them to the pan.

Preheat the oven to 230°C (450°F or Mark 8).

Add the canned tomatoes and their juice, the sugar, onion, ginger and garlic to the potatoes and bring the mixture to the boil. Reduce the heat and simmer the mixture, stirring frequently, until it has thickened and most of the liquid has evaporated – 15 to 20 minutes.

While the tomato mixture is simmering, prepare the fresh tomato. With a small sharp knife, cut the flesh of the tomato away from the seeds and core. Discard the seeds and core. Then cut the flesh into 5 mm (¼ inch) dice and put into a large bowl. Lightly oil a 1.5 litre

(2½ pint) soufflé dish and add the flour. Invert the dish and shake out the excess flour.

Transfer the cooked tomato mixture to a food processor or blender and purée it. Pour the purée into the bowl with the diced tomato and stir in the egg yolk, salt, some pepper and the olive oil. Set the bowl aside.

Beat the egg whites in a bowl until they form soft peaks. Stir about a quarter of the beaten whites into the tomato mixture to lighten it. Gently fold in the remaining whites just until they are blended in.

Pour the soufflé mixture into the prepared dish and bake it until the soufflé has risen and the top is dark brown – 30 to 40 minutes. Serve the soufflé immediately.

Stuffed Eggs and Celery

Makes 60 pieces

Working (and total) time: about 40 minutes

Per piece:
Calories 15
Protein 1g
Cholesterol 10mg
Total fat 1g
Saturated fat trace
Sodium 30mg

6	eggs	6
8	sticks celery	8
1	small sweet red pepper, skinned, seeded and deribbed	1
1	small sweet green pepper, skinned, seeded and deribbed	1
125 g	low-fat ricotta cheese	4 oz
100 g	fromage frais	3½ oz
¼ tsp	salt	¼ tsp
	freshly ground black pepper	
3 tbsp	finely cut fresh chives	3 tbsp

Put the eggs into a saucepan and cover with cold water. Bring the water to the boil and cook the eggs gently for 10 minutes. Immediately, pour off the boiling water and cool the eggs under cold running water.

Meanwhile, prepare the vegetables. Trim, wash and dry celery sticks. Cut the sticks into 15 cm (6 inch) evenly shaped lengths. Cut half of the red pepper into fine strips; reserve 12 strips and chop the rest into small dice. Cut one third of the green pepper into dice of the same size. (The remainder of the peppers will not be needed for this recipe.)

Shell the eggs, cut each one in half lengthwise and remove the yolks. Sieve the egg yolks through a nylon sieve into a bowl, then sieve the

ricotta cheese through the same sieve into the bowl. Add the *fromage frais*, salt and some pepper, and 2 tablespoons of the chives. Beat well together until smooth and creamy.

Put the egg mixture into a piping bag fitted with a medium-size star nozzle. Pipe a whirl of mixture into each egg white, then pipe the rest into the celery.

Sprinkle the eggs with the remaining chives and garnish each one with a twisted strip of red pepper. Sprinkle half of the celery with the chopped red pepper and the other half with the green pepper. Cut the celery into 2.5 cm (1 inch) lengths. Arrange the eggs and celery on serving platters.

Egg and Watercress Canapés

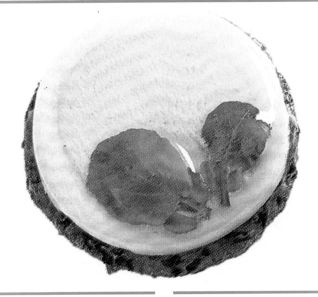

**Makes 12
canapés**

**Working
time: about
30 minutes**

**Total time;
about
1 hour and
15 minutes
(includes
cooling and
setting)**

Per canapé

Calories
35

Protein
2g

Cholesterol
40mg

Total fat
2g

Saturated fat
trace

Sodium
70mg

3	eggs	**3**	**⅛ tsp**	salt	**⅛ tsp**
3 or 4	thin slices rye bread	**3 or 4**		freshly ground black pepper	
15 g	polyunsaturated margarine	**½ oz**	**15 cl**	vegetable aspic, melted	**¼ pint**
1 tbsp	finely chopped watercress leaves, plus 12 whole watercress leaves	**1 tbsp**			

Put the eggs into a saucepan and cover with cold water. Bring to the boil, then cook them gently for 10 minutes. Immediately, pour off the boiling water and cool the eggs under cold running water. Carefully remove the shells.

Using a 4 cm (1¾ inch) diameter plain round cutter, cut 12 rounds from the rye bread. Put the margarine, chopped watercress, salt and some pepper into a small bowl. Beat until smooth, then spread thinly over each round of rye bread.

Using an egg slicer, slice the eggs. Choose the 12 best slices and place one on each round of bread. (Use the remaining slices in a salad.)

Dip each whole watercress leaf in the aspic and place one leaf on each canapé. Place the canapés on a wire rack over a large tray and refrigerate for about 5 minutes to set. Stir the remaining aspic over ice, or refrigerate, until it begins to thicken. Carefully spoon the aspic over the canapés to coat them evenly. Refrigerate until set firm – about 20 minutes. Keep the canapés refrigerated until just before serving.

Pink Trout Mousse

Serves 12
as a
first course

Working
time: about
30 minutes

Total time:
about
4 hours
(includes
chilling)

Calories
75

Protein
12g

Cholesterol
25mg

Total fat
2g

Saturated fat
trace

Sodium
120mg

2	shallots, finely chopped	2
30 cl	unsalted fish stock	$\frac{1}{2}$ pint
$\frac{1}{2}$	lime, juice only	$\frac{1}{2}$
2 tbsp	dry vermouth	2 tbsp
500 g	trout fillets	1 lb
1 tbsp	tomato paste	1 tbsp

90 g	thick Greek yogurt	3 oz
$\frac{1}{2}$ tsp	salt	$\frac{1}{2}$ tsp
	white pepper	
1 tbsp	powdered gelatine	1 tbsp
3	egg whites	3
$\frac{1}{4}$	cucumber, sliced, for garnish	$\frac{1}{4}$

Place the shallots in a large, shallow pan with the fish stock, lime juice and vermouth. Bring the liquid to the boil, reduce the heat and simmer gently for 3 minutes, until the shallots have softened. Lay the trout fillets in the stock, skin side down. Cover the pan and simmer gently for 3 minutes, then remove the pan from the heat and leave the fish to cool in the stock.

Remove the fish from the pan with a slotted spoon. Roughly flake the fish, discarding the skin and any bones. Strain the stock. Place the fish in a food processor or blender, together with the strained stock, and blend the ingredients until smooth. Turn out the mixture into a bowl and beat in the tomato paste, yogurt, salt and some pepper.

Dissolve the gelatine in 3 tablespoons of cold water. Slowly pour the dissolved gelatine over the fish mixture, beating it well all the time. Chill the fish mixture until it is just beginning to set – 15 to 20 minutes.

Whisk the egg whites until they are stiff but not dry. Using a large metal spoon, stir one third of the egg whites into the fish mixture to lighten it, then gently fold in the remaining egg whites; avoid overmixing. Turn the mousse into a dampened serving dish and chill it until set – about 3 hours.

Serve the mousse garnished with the cucumber.

Suggested accompaniment: granary toast.

Haddock Terrine with Dill

Serves 16
as a first
course

Working
time: about
45 minutes

Total time:
about
5 hours
(includes
chilling)

Calories
70

Protein
11g

Cholesterol
30mg

Total fat
2g

Saturated fat
trace

Sodium
295mg

90 g	fine fresh white breadcrumbs	3 oz
25 cl	skimmed milk	8 fl oz
275 g	boned and skinned smoked Finnan haddock, cut into pieces	9 oz
300 g	boned and skinned fresh haddock, cut into pieces	10 oz
1	egg	1
3	egg whites	3

1 tbsp	dry white vermouth	1 tbsp
$\frac{1}{2}$ tsp	finely grated lemon rind	$\frac{1}{2}$ tsp
$1\frac{1}{2}$ tbsp	fresh lemon juice	$1\frac{1}{2}$ tbsp
$2\frac{1}{2}$ tbsp	chopped parsley	$2\frac{1}{2}$ tbsp
3 tbsp	chopped fresh basil	3 tbsp
30 cl	vegetable aspic, melted	$\frac{1}{2}$ pint
3	quail's eggs, hard boiled (optional)	3

Preheat the oven to 180°C (350°F or Mark 4). Soak 60 g (2 oz) of the breadcrumbs in milk in a bowl. Purée smoked haddock and 275 g (6 oz) of fresh haddock with the egg, two of the egg whites, vermouth, lemon rind and juice, and the milk soaked breadcrumbs. Set aside.

Purée remaining fresh haddock, egg white and breadcrumbs, parsley and 2 tablespoons of dill.

Line a 15 by 10 by 7.5 cm (6 by 4 by 3 inch) terrine or loaf tin with parchment paper. Spoon half of the smoked haddock purée into the terrine. Smooth the top of the mixture. Carefully place the herbed fresh haddock mixture down the centre of the smoked haddock purée. (The herbed mixture will sink slightly into the smoked

haddock purée.) Carefully spread the remaining smoked haddock purée on top.

Cover the terrine and stand it in a large roasting pan. Pour in enough boiling water to come two thirds of the way up the side of the terrine. Bake the terrine until a skewer inserted in the centre is hot to the touch – 1 to $1\frac{1}{4}$ hours. Pour off any excess liquid. Leave to cool – about 1 hour – then refrigerate for 2 hours.

Pour a thin layer of aspic over surface and chill until almost set – about 10 minutes. Press remaining dill lightly into aspic and chill until completely set. Decorate with quail's eggs and pour over remaining aspic. Chill to set.

Individual Tomato Pizzas

Serves 4

Working time: about 45 minutes

Total time: about 3 hours (includes rising and cooling)

Calories 345
Protein 10g
Cholesterol 55mg
Total fat 9g
Saturated fat 3g
Sodium 135mg

250 g	strong white flour	8 oz
¼ tsp	salt	¼ tsp
15 g	unsalted butter	½ oz
1 tsp	easy-blend dried yeast	1 tsp
1 tbsp	safflower oil	1 tbsp
250 g	onions, thinly sliced	8 oz
2	garlic cloves, crushed	2
500 g	tomatoes, skinned and sliced	1 lb
1 tbsp	tomato paste	1 tbsp
1 tbsp	chopped fresh basil, or 1 tsp dried basil	1 tbsp
1 tsp	chopped fresh marjoram, or ¼ tsp dried marjoram	1 tsp
90 g	button mushrooms, trimmed and sliced	3 oz
	freshly ground black pepper	
¼	sweet green pepper, seeded deribbed, blanched for 2 minutes and cut into long, narrow strips	¼
4	quail's eggs, hard boiled, each cut into four slices (optional)	4
1	large black olive, stoned and cut into thin slivers	1

Sift flour and half salt into a bowl, rub in the butter. Mix in the yeast. Mix sufficient warm water – about 15 cl (¼ pint) – into the dry ingredients to form a pliable dough. Knead dough on a floured surface, for 5 to 10 minutes, until smooth. Put into a large bowl and cover with a towel. Put dough in a warm place to rise for about 1 hour, until doubled in size.

Fry the onions and garlic gently in the oil until soft and lightly coloured. Add tomatoes and paste, and cook for another 5 to 8 minutes. Add the herbs, the mushrooms, the remaining salt and some pepper, and cook for a further 1 to 2 minutes. Cool.

Grease four 15 to 18 cm (6 to 7 inch) flan tins. Knead the dough, and divide into quarters, and press each piece to fit a tin and spread with tomato mixture. Preheat the oven to 220°C (420°F or Mark 7), and leave pizzas to rise – 10 minutes.

Bake pizzas for 20 minutes, then decorate with peppers, eggs and olives.

Asparagus and Walnut Frittata

Serves 6

Working
(and total)
time: about
30 minutes

Calories
150

Protein
10g

Cholesterol
120mg

Total fat
10g

Saturated fat
3g

Sodium
205mg

300 g	asparagus, trimmed	10 oz		45 g	shelled walnuts, toasted and chopped	1½ oz
3	eggs	3		1 tbsp	chopped fresh basil	1 tbsp
3	egg whites	3		⅛ tsp	salt	⅛ tsp
45 g	Parmesan cheese, freshly grated	1½ oz			freshly ground black pepper	
60 g	day-old wholemeal bread, crusts removed, soaked for 10 minutes in 4 tbsp skimmed milk	2 oz		1 tsp	virgin olive or safflower oil	1 tsp

Bring a large, shallow pan of water to the boil. Cook the asparagus in the boiling water for about 2 minutes, then drain it, refresh it under cold running water, and drain it again well. Cut the asparagus into 5 cm (2 inch) pieces and set them aside.

Whisk the whole eggs and egg whites with the Parmesan and the chopped walnuts. Add the soaked bread, the basil and the asparagus pieces to the egg mixture, and season it with the salt and some black pepper. Mix the ingredients well.

Heat the oil in a non-stick frying pan over medium heat and pour in the egg mixture;

distribute the asparagus pieces evenly in the frying pan and flatten the mixture with the back of a wooden spoon. Cook the frittata over medium heat for 5 to 8 minutes, until the underside is firm. Invert the frittata on to a large plate, then slide it back into the frying pan and cook the second side until it, too, is firm and golden-brown – another 5 to 8 minutes. Slide the frittata back on to the plate and serve hot or leave to cool.

Suggested accompaniment: a salad of mixed lettuce leaves dressed with a light vinaigrette.

Individual Smoked Trout Flans

Makes 6 flans

Working time: about 25 minutes

Total time: about 1 hour and 10 minutes

Per flan:

Calories
160

Protein
22g

Cholesterol
55mg

Total fat
15g

Saturated fat
3g

Sodium
210mg

175 g	wholemeal flour	**6 oz**
90 g	polyunsaturated margarine, chilled	**3 oz**
400 g	skinned smoked trout fillets	**14 oz**
15 cl	skimmed milk	**¼ pint**
3 tbsp	grated horseradish	**3 tbsp**
125 g	low-fat fromage frais	**4 oz**
1 tbsp	chopped fresh tarragon	**1 tbsp**

125 g	cucumber, peeled, seeded and finely diced	**4 oz**
1	lemon, finely grated rind and juice freshly ground black pepper	**1**
2	egg whites	**2**
6	lemon wedges, for garnish	**6**
6	tarragon sprigs, for garnish	**6**

Put the flour into a large bowl and rub the margarine into the flour, until the mixture resembles fine breadcrumbs. Stir in 3 tablespoons of cold water to make a firm dough. Knead dough on a floured surface until smooth. Divide the dough into six portions. Roll out the portions thinly and use them to line six fluted flan cases about 10 cm (4 inches) in diameter and 2.5 cm (1 inch) deep. Prick the bases and sides with a fork and chill for 20 minutes. Preheat oven to 200°C (400°F or Mark 6).

Place the trout fillets in a large saucepan with the milk, and poach gently until the fish is tender and flakes easily with a fork – about 15 minutes. Drain and discard the milk. Set the fish aside and leave it to cool.

Bake the flan cases for 20 to 25 minutes, until lightly browned. Reduce the oven temperature to 170°C (325°F or mark 3).

Flake the flesh of the trout and mix with the horseradish, *fromage frais*, cucumber, chopped tarragon, the lemon rind and juice and some black pepper, and mix well.

In a separate bowl, whisk the egg whites lightly until they begin to form soft peaks. Fold the whites into the fish mixture. Fill the pastry cases and bake the flans until they are set – about 15 minutes. Allow the flans to cool completely in their tins, then refrigerate until required. Garnish with lemon and tarragon.

Courgette and Camembert Quiche

Serves 8

Working time: about 30 minutes

Total time: about 1 hour and 35 minutes

Calories 250

Protein 8g

Cholesterol 70mg

Total fat 13g

Saturated fat 3g

Sodium 3mg

600 g	courgettes, sliced	1¼ lb
1 tsp	polyunsaturated margarine	1 tsp
1	onion, finely chopped	1
1½ tbsp	chopped fresh basil, or 1½ tsp dried basil	1½ tbsp
140 g	firm Camembert, rind removed cut into small pieces	4½ oz
30 cl	skimmed milk	½ pint

2	eggs, beaten	2
⅛ tsp	salt	⅛ tsp
	freshly ground black pepper	
	Shortcrust Pastry	
200 g	plain flour	7 oz
⅛ tsp	salt	⅛ tsp
90 g	polyunsaturated margarine, chilled	3 oz

Preheat oven to 180°C (350°F or Mark 4). Place courgettes in an oiled baking dish, cover with foil and bake until tender – about 20 minutes.

Meanwhile, sift the flour and salt into a bowl, rub in margarine until mixture resembles fine breadcrumbs. Stir in 3 to 4 tablespoons of cold water to make a firm dough. Knead dough on a floured surface until smooth. Roll out the dough and use it to line a 2.5 cm (1 inch) deep 22 cm (9 inch) flan dish. Prick the base and sides with a fork and chill the case for 20 minutes.

Increase oven temperature to 200°C (400°F or Mark 6). Bake pastry case for 15 minutes, then remove from the oven. Reduce the oven temperature to 180°C (350°F or Mark 4).

Gently fry the onion in margarine until it is transparent – 5 to 6 minutes. Add the basil and cook for another minute.

Spread half of onion mixture in the base of the flan case and cover it with half of the courgettes, then add remaining onion, followed by rest of courgettes. Sprinkle the diced cheese on top. In a bowl, whisk together the milk, eggs, salt and some black pepper. Pour this mixture over the layered vegetables. Bake the quiche until it is set and golden-brown – 30 to 40 minutes. Serve ho' or cold.

Mussel and Leek Quiche

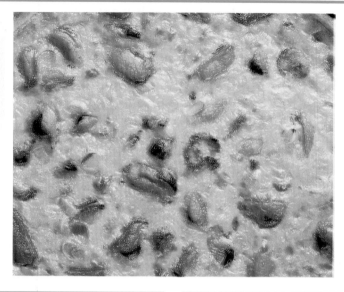

Serves 12		Calories 150
Working time: about 40 minutes		Protein 10g
		Cholesterol 80mg
Total time: about 3 hours (includes chilling)		Total fat 6g
		Saturated fat 2g
		Sodium 135mg

1.5 kg	mussels, scrubbed and debearded	**3 lb**
175 g	baby leeks, trimmed to leave 5 cm (2 inches) of green stem, sliced into rings	**6 oz**
30 cl	dry white wine	**½ pint**
1 tsp	saffron threads, crushed	**1 tsp**
2	eggs	**2**

1	egg yolk	**1**
2 tbsp	crème fraîche	**2 tbsp**
15 cl	skimmed milk	**¼ pint**
	Yogurt Pastry	
140 g	plain flour	**4½ oz**
45 g	polyunsaturated margarine, chilled	**1½ oz**
90 g	thick Greek yogurt	**3 oz**

Rub margarine into flour until fine crumbs are formed. Add yogurt and mix to form a firm, slightly wet ball. Scrape down the sides of the bowl and gather all the dough into one ball. Wrap the dough in plastic film and chill for 1 hour.

Grease a 25 cm (10 inch) loose-bottomed flan tin. Place the dough in the tin. Gently flatten and spread the dough to line the tin, pressing it into a smooth, even layer over the base and sides. Refrigerate until ready to fill.

Bring to boil mussels, leeks and wine in a large pan, then cover and steam the mussels for 3 to 5 minutes, or until shells have opened, shaking the pan occasionally. Strain through muslin, reserving the liquid. Pour reserved liquid into a clean pan and add the saffron threads.

Reduce by boiling to ¼ litre (8 fl oz), then set aside to cool. Remove the mussels from their shells, discarding any that have not opened.

Preheat the oven to 180°C (350°F or Mark 4). In a jug, beat the eggs and egg yolk and whisk in the *creme fraîche*. Add the cooled saffron liquid and the skimmed milk to the jug and whisk thoroughly.

Arrange the mussels and leeks evenly in the chilled flan case, and pour on the saffron custard. Place the quiche in the oven and immediately increase the setting to 200°C (400°F or Mark 6). Bake for 15 minutes, then reduce heat to 180°C (350°F or Mark 4) and cook for a further 25 minutes until custard is set. Serve hot or cold.

Pink and Green Fish Terrine

**Serves 16
as a
first course**

**Working
time: about
45 minutes**

**Total time:
about
4 hours
(includes
chilling)**

Calories
50
Protein
7g
Cholesterol
30mg
Total fat
2g
Saturated fat
1g
Sodium
85mg

500 g	pink trout fillets, skinned	**1 lb**
1½ tsp	chopped wild fennel	**1½ tsp**
1½ tsp	chopped fresh dill	**1½ tsp**
4	egg whites	**4**
½ tsp	salt	**½ tsp**
	white pepper	

15 g	unsalted butter	**½ oz**
90 g	parsley, stalks removed	**3 oz**
500 g	whiting or haddock fillets, skinned	**1 lb**
1 tbsp	chopped fresh tarragon, or 1 tsp dried tarragon	**1 tbsp**
1 tbsp	dry sherry or vermouth	**1 tbsp**

Line a 20 by 6 by 7.5 cm (8 by 2½ by 3 inch) terrine or loaf tin with parchment paper.

Roughly chop the trout fillets, then purée them in a food processor. Add the fennel, dill, two of the egg whites, ¼ teaspoon of the salt and some white pepper, and blend again to form a smooth paste. Transfer the pink paste to the prepared terrine, smoothing it down with the back of a spoon, then make a deep groove lengthwise down the centre. Chill the paste while you prepare the green layer.

Preheat the oven to 190°C (375°F or Mark 5). Melt the butter in a small saucepan, add the parsley and cook it over low heat until it is soft – about 10 minutes. Allow the parsley to cool, then place it in the food processor. Roughly chop the white fish and add it to the parsley. Process the parsley and fish until well blended. Add the tarragon, the remaining egg whites, the sherry, the remaining salt and some white pepper. Process the mixture to a smooth purée. Transfer the purée to the terrine and smooth it into an even layer with the back of a spoon.

Cover the terrine with non-stick parchment paper and stand it in a large roasting pan or dish. Pour boiling water into the roasting pan to come two thirds of the way up the side of the terrine. Bake the terrine until the mixture is set and firm to the touch – about 35 minutes. Leave the terrine to cool, then chill it for at least 2 hours. Turn out the terrine on to a platter, and serve it cut into slices.

Marbled Carrot and Courgette Soufflé

Serves 12
as a
side dish

Working
time: about
45 minutes

Total time:
about
1 hour and
30 minutes

Calories
90

Protein
6g

Cholesterol
30mg

Total fat
4g

Saturated fat
2g

Sodium
170mg

1 kg	carrots, peeled and sliced into 5 mm (¼ inch) rounds	2 lb
2	medium onions, coarsely chopped plus 45 g (1½ oz) finely chopped	2
15 g	unsalted butter	½ oz
750 g	courgettes, seeded and grated freshly ground black pepper	1½ lb
12.5 cl	semi-skimmed milk	4 fl oz
125 g	Parmesan or Romano cheese, freshly grated	4 oz
1 tsp	sugar	1 tsp
1	egg yolk	1
5	egg whites	5

Butter a 2 litre (3½ pint) soufflé dish and flour it lightly. Refrigerate.

Steam the carrots and onions until the carrots are very soft – about 20 minutes.

While carrots are steaming, fry the finely chopped onion, then the courgettes and some pepper in the butter. Cook, stirring frequently, until liquid has evaporated – 5 to 7 minutes. Transfer the mixture to a bowl. Stir in 6 cl (2 fl oz) of the milk and 45 g (1½ oz) of the cheese.

Purée carrots and onions then add the remaining milk and sugar; purée the mixture for 1 minute more. Transfer to a large bowl, add the egg yolk, 60 g (2 oz) of the cheese and some pepper, and mix well.

Preheat the oven to 230°C (450°F or Mark 7). In a clean, dry metal bowl, beat the egg whites until soft peaks form; do not overbeat them. Fold one quarter of the whites into the carrot mixture and blend well. Fold another quarter of the whites into the courgette mixture and blend well. Gently fold half of the remaining whites into the carrot mixture; the whites should not be completely incorporated. Repeat the process with remaining whites and courgette mixture.

Pour the two vegetable mixtures into opposite sides of the soufflé dish. Place a spoon in the middle of the courgette mixture and swirl it three quarters of the way round the soufflé to marble. Bake for 45 minutes until golden-brown. Serve immediately.

Terrine of Butternut Squash and Egg Noodles

Serves 12
as a dish

Working
time: about
40 minutes

Total time:
about
1 hour and
15 minutes

Calories
190

Protein
6g

Cholesterol
45mg

Total fat
5g

Saturated fat
2g

Sodium
200mg

300 g	wide egg noodles	**10 oz**		1 tsp	ground allspice	**1 tsp**
¾ tsp	salt	**¾ tsp**			freshly ground black pepper	
½ tsp	ground cinnamon	**½ tsp**		**2 tbsp**	safflower oil	**2 tbsp**
½ tsp	ground coriander	**½ tsp**		**1**	onion, finely chopped	**1**
1.25 kg	butternut squash or pumpkin,	**2½ lb**		**1**	egg, and 3 egg whites, lightly	**1**
	peeled, halved lengthwise and				beaten	
	seeded, cut into 5 mm (¼ inch) slices			**15 g**	unsalted butter	**½ oz**

Preheat the oven to 180°C (350°F or Mark 4). Combine the salt, spices and some pepper in a bowl. Brush squash with 1 tablespoon of oil, arrange in a single layer on a baking sheet. Sprinkle with half spice mixture and bake until softened – about 15 minutes. Leave oven on.

Bring 2 litres (3½ pints) of water with 1 teaspoon of salt to the boil. Pour remainder of oil into a frying pan over medium heat. Add onion and some more pepper and cook until onion is translucent – about 7 minutes. Meanwhile, boil noodles until they are almost *al dente* – about 7 minutes.

Drain noodles and return to pan. Add egg and egg whites along with the remaining spice mixture. Add the butter, 4 tablespoons of water and the onion, and stir until the butter is melted.

Butter a 23 by 12.5 cm (9 by 5 inch) loaf pan. Line the bottom and sides with squash slices, covering all surfaces completely; reserve about one third of the slices for the top. Add noodle mixture and press it down. Arrange reserved squash evenly over the top and cover with a piece of greaseproof paper. Put a heavy, flat-bottomed object, on top of the paper to weight the contents down, then bake the terrine for 35 minutes. Let the terrine stand for 10 minutes before unmoulding it. Serve hot or cold.

Tossed Salad with Eggs and French Beans

Serves 6

Working time: about 15 minutes

Total time: about 40 minutes (includes marinating)

Calories 115
Protein 3g
Cholesterol 75mg
Total fat 10g
Saturated fat 2g
Sodium 100mg

½	small red onion, cut thinly into rings	½
1	small red lollo lettuce, washed and dried, leaves torn	1
30 g	rocket, washed and dried	1 oz
90 g	French beans, topped and blanched for 3 minutes in boiling water	3 oz
2	eggs, hard boiled, each cut into six wedges	2
6	black olives	6
3	red basil sprigs	3
3	green basil sprigs	3
	Vinaigrette Dressing	
1	garlic clove, crushed	1
¼ tsp	salt	¼ tsp
	freshly ground black pepper	
1 tbsp	red wine vinegar	1 tbsp
3 tbsp	virgin olive oil	3 tbsp

First prepare the vinaigrette. Place the garlic, salt and some pepper in a large salad bowl. Using a wooden pestle, pound the ingredients until they break down into a paste. Add the vinegar and stir until the salt disolves. Pour in the olive oil and mix thoroughly.

With your hands or the pestle, stir the onion slices into the vinaigrette to coat them well. Set them aside to marinate for 30 minutes.

Cross a pair of salad servers over the bottom of the bowl, to keep the dressing separate from the leaves that will be added before the salad is tossed. Lay a few of the largest lettuce leaves on the servers, then fill the bowl with the remaining lettuce and the rocket.

Top the leaves with the French beans, hard boiled eggs, olives and basil. Draw out the servers from the bed of lettuce and rocket and toss the salad with the servers, or by hand, until all its ingredients are lightly coated with the dressing.

Artichokes with an Egg and Herb Vinaigrette

Serves 6

Working time: about 20 minutes

Total time: about 1 hour

Calories 100

Protein 2g

Cholesterol 35mg

Total fat 8g

Saturated fat 1g

Sodium 20mg

6	artichokes, trimmed, chokes	**6**
1	egg, hard-boiled	**1**
1 tbsp	white wine vinegar	**1 tbsp**
½ tsp	fresh lemon juice	**½ tsp**
3 tbsp	virgin olive oil	**3 tbsp**
¼ tsp	salt	**¼ tsp**

	freshly ground black pepper	
1 tbsp	chopped parsley	**1 tbsp**
1 tsp	chopped lemon balm	**1 tsp**
1 tsp	finely cut chives	**1 tsp**
1 tsp	torn summer savory leaves	**1 tsp**

In a large, saucepan, bring 5 litres (8½ pints) of water to the boil. Add the artichokes and 1 tablespoon of salt, and boil the artichokes until they are tender – about 40 minutes. Place a colander over a bowl and drain the artichokes, reserving 2 tablespoons of their cooking water.

While the artichokes are cooling, shell the hard-boiled egg and chop it coarsely. In a small bowl, whisk together the vinegar, lemon juice, reserved cooking water from the artichokes, olive oil, the ¼ teaspoon of salt and some black pepper. When the dressing is thoroughly combined, stir in the chopped egg, parsley, lemon balm, chives and summer savory.

Place the cooled artichokes on individual serving plates. Divide the herb dressing among the hollowed-out centres, and serve the artichokes.

Editor's Note: The easiest way to eat artichokes presented in this manner is to break off the outer leaves first and use them to scoop out the dressing. When the leaves are finished, use a knife and fork to eat the tender artichoke bottoms, with the remaining herb vinaigrette. Each diner should be supplied with a finger bowl.

Crab and Paprika Soufflés

Serves 6

Working time: about 15 minutes

Total time: about 35 minutes

Calories
55
Protein
8g
Cholesterol
55mg
Total fat
2g
Saturated fat
1g
Sodium
150mg

175 g	cooked crab meat, picked over, chilled	**6 oz**
1	egg yolk	**1**
½ tsp	fresh lemon juice	**½ tsp**

175 g	fromage frais	**6 oz**
2 tsp	paprika	**2 tsp**
¼ tsp	salt	**¼ tsp**
5	egg whites	**5**

Preheat the oven to 180°C (350°F or Mark 4).

In a large bowl, combine the chilled crab meat, egg yolk, lemon juice and *fromage frais*. Add the paprika and the salt to the mixture.

Whisk the egg whites until they are stiff but not dry, then fold them gently into the crab meat mixture. Divide the mixture among six 12.5 cl (4 fl oz) very lightly oiled ramekin dishes and place them in a baking tin. Bake the soufflés until they are lightly set and golden-coloured – about 17 minutes – and serve immediately.

Tomato Sirloin Loaf

Serves 8
as a
main course

Working
time: about
20 minutes

Total time:
about
8 hours
(includes
chilling)

Calories
285

Protein
27g

Cholesterol
50mg

Total fat
12g

Saturated fat
4g

Sodium
300mg

2 tbsp	virgin olive oil	2 tbsp
2	onions, finely chopped	2
400 g	canned plum tomatoes, chopped	14 oz
1 tbsp	fresh oregano, or 1 tsp dried oregano	1 tbsp
1 tsp	lightly crushed fennel seeds	1 tsp
¼ tsp	salt	¼ tsp
	freshly ground black pepper	

750 g	beef sirloin, trimmed of fat and minced	1½ lb
3	garlic cloves, finely chopped	3
30 g	parsley, chopped	1 oz
1 tsp	Tabasco sauce	1 tsp
2 tsp	Worcester sauce	2 tsp
175 g	dry breadcrumbs	6 oz
3	egg whites	3

Heat 1 tablespoon of the oil in a saucepan over medium-low heat. Add half of onion, stir, then cover and cook the onion until it has softened – about 5 minutes. Add tomatoes, oregano, fennel seeds, salt and a little pepper. Simmer uncovered, stirring occasionally, until it has reduced to about 30 cl (½ pint) – about 40 minutes. Sieve.

Preheat the oven to 180°C (350°F or Mark 4). Brush a 20 by 12 by 7.5 cm (8 by 5 by 3 inch) loaf tin with some of the remaining olive oil.

Put the sirloin in a bowl with the tomato sauce. Mix in the garlic, the remaining onion, the parsley, Tabasco sauce, Worcester sauce and plenty of freshly ground black pepper. Add the breadcrumbs and mix well. Finally, add the egg whites and blend them thoroughly into the mixture with your hands.

Form the mixture into a smooth fat sausage shape and lay it in the tin, pressing it down firmly on all sides. Brush the top of the loaf with the remaining olive oil, then cover it with foil. Bake until cooked through and a skewer inserted into the middle is hot to touch when withdrawn – about 1 hour.

Leave the loaf to cool to room temperature – about 2 hours – refrigerate for at least 4 hours before serving.

Suggested accompaniments: boiled new potatoes; steamed asparagus spears.

Spanish Omelette

Serves 4		**Calories** 190
Working time: about 20 minutes		**Protein** 7g
		Cholesterol 110mg
Total time: about 35 minutes		**Total fat** 10g
		Saturated fat 2g
		Sodium 260mg

2 tbsp	virgin olive oil	**2 tbsp**
1	onion, chopped	**1**
2	garlic cloves, chopped	**2**
2	small courgettes (about 125 g/4 oz), trimmed and thinly sliced	**2**
½ tsp	salt	**½ tsp**
	freshly ground black pepper	
1	large potato (about 300 g/10 oz), peeled, cooked in boiling water for 25 to 30 minutes, drained and coarsely chopped	**1**

2	eggs	**2**
2	egg whites	**2**
125 g	French beans, trimmed, cooked in boiling water for 5 minutes, drained, refreshed under cold running water and cut into 2.5 cm (1 inch) lengths	**4 oz**
2	tomatoes (about 175 g/6 oz), skinned, seeded and chopped	**2**
½ tbsp	chopped fresh oregano, or ½ tsp dried oregano	**½ tbsp**

Heat 1½ tablespoons of the oil in a heavy frying pan over medium heat. Add the onion and fry until it is soft – about 3 minutes. Add the garlic and courgettes, cover the pan and cook the vegetables gently for 10 minutes, stirring them occasionally. Remove the pan from the heat.

In a large bowl, beat together the eggs and egg whites, the salt and some black pepper. Add the fried vegetables, the potato, beans, tomatoes and oregano, and stir gently to mix the ingredients.

Heat the remaining oil in a 25 cm (10 inch) non-stick frying pan and pour in the egg mixture. Cook the omelette gently over medium heat for 3 to 4 minutes, until the underside is pale golden. Place the frying pan under a preheated medium-hot grill and cook the omelette for a further 2 to 3 minutes, or until it is lightly set. Cut into quarters and serve.

Suggested accompaniment: mixed salad.

Pumpkin Soufflé

Serves 4

Working time: about 30 minutes

Total time: about 2 hour and 45 minutes

Calories 200

Protein 11g

Cholesterol 85mg

Total fat 12g

Saturated fat 6g

Sodium 300mg

750 g	slice of pumpkin, seeds removed	1½ lb
2 tbsp	dry breadcrumbs	2 tbsp
30 g	unsalted butter	1 oz
2 tbsp	plain flour	2 tbsp
12.5 cl	skimmed milk	4 fl oz
1	egg yolk	1
¼ tsp	salt	¼ tsp
1 tsp	ground cinnamon	1 tsp
3 tbsp	freshly grated Parmesan cheese	3 tbsp
5	egg whites	5

Preheat the oven to 190°C (375°F or Mark 5).

Wrap the pumpkin in a sheet of foil and place it on a baking sheet. Bake it in the oven for about 1 hour, until it is soft. Check the pumpkin after this time; if it is still hard, return it to the oven until soft. When the pumpkin is ready, allow it to cool, uncovered.

Meanwhile, grease a 90 cl (1½ pint) soufflé dish and dust the base and sides with the breadcrumbs. Reduce the oven temperature to 200°C (400°F or Mark 6).

Scoop all the pumpkin pulp from the skin and pass the pulp through a nylon sieve; there should be about 35 g (12 oz) of sieved pumpkin. Put the pumpkin in a saucepan and, stirring continuously, dry out the pulp over medium heat until it becomes fairly dense and is no longer wet –

about 10 minutes. Set the pumpkin aside.

In a small, heavy-bottomed saucepan, melt the butter over gentle heat. Remove the pan from the heat. Stir in the flour, then stir in the milk a little at a time. Return the pan to the heat and cook the mixture for about 30 seconds, stirring constantly, until it thickens. Take the pan off the heat again and stir in the egg yolk, followed by the pumpkin, salt, cinnamon and 2 tablespoons of the Parmesan. Set the mixture aside.

Whisk egg whites until they hold their shape; using a metal spoon, fold gently into the pumpkin mixture. Turn the mixture into prepared soufflé dish and sprinkle with remaining Parmesan.

Bake soufflé in the oven for about 40 minutes, until it is well risen and set. Serve immediately.

Scandinavian Salad

Serves 6

Working time: about 45 minutes

Total time: about 2 hours and 15 minutes (includes chilling)

Calories 195
Protein 7g
Cholesterol 75mg
Total fat 4g
Saturated fat 1g
Sodium 190mg

750 g	small beetroots, washed and trimmed, 5 cm (2 inch) stem left on each	1½ lb
750 g	new potatoes, lightly scrubbed, halved if large	1½ lb
2	eggs, hard-boiled	2
1 tbsp	red wine vinegar	1 tbsp
1 tsp	molasses	1 tsp
2 tbsp	thick Greek yogurt	2 tbsp
1 tsp	caraway seeds, lightly toasted freshly ground black pepper	1 tsp

	curly endive leaves, for garnish	
	Mustard dressing	
2 tsp	mild Dijon mustard	2 tsp
1 tsp	dry mustard	1 tsp
1 tsp	yellow mustard seeds, toasted	1 tsp
½ tsp	freshly grated horseradish	½ tsp
1 tsp	white wine vinegar	1 tsp
2 tsp	virgin olive oil	2 tsp
15 cl	plain low-fat yogurt	¼ pint
2 tbsp	finely chopped fresh dill	2 tbsp

Preheat the oven to 200°C (400°F or Mark 6). Wrap beetroots, in a single package, in aluminum foil. Bake until they are tender - about 1 hour. When cool enough to handle, peel, removing stems, and cut into 1 cm (½ inch) cubes. Place in a large bowl.

While the beetroots are cooking, steam the new potatoes until they are just tender – 15 to 20 minutes.

Cut 1 hard-boiled egg lengthwise into 6 wedges. Set aside. Slice the second in half. Reserve the yolk; dice the white finely and set it aside for garnish.

Put the red wine vinegar in a small bowl, add the molasses and stir until smooth. Pour over the beetroot cubes and toss thoroughly. Add yogurt, caraway seeds and some black pepper. Stir thoroughly, then set the bowl aside.

Sieve the reserved egg yolk into a bowl and blend in the Dijon mustard. Add the dry mustard, mustard seeds and grated horseradish, stir thoroughly. Blend in the white wine vinegar, followed by the oil. Mix in the yogurt and chopped dill.

Cube the potatoes and place them in a large bowl. Pour on the mustard dressing and toss. Serve beetroot and potatoes in a bowl lined with endive (as illustration) leaves; sprinkled with chopped egg.

Jerusalem Artichoke and Walnut Soufflés

Serves 4

Working
time: about
20 minutes

Total time;
about
45 minutes

Calories
145
Protein
8g
Cholesterol
60mg
Total fat
10g
Saturated fat
2g
Sodium
290mg

250 g	Jerusalem artichokes, peeled and cut into small pieces	8 oz
2 tsp	cornflour	2 tsp
15 cl	skimmed milk	¼ pint
¼ tsp	ground mace	¼ tsp
½ tsp	salt	½ tsp

3 tbsp	chopped parsley	3 tbsp
	freshly ground black pepper	
60 g	shelled walnuts, finely chopped	2 oz
1	egg yolk	1
3	egg whites	3
1 tbsp	freshly grated Parmesan cheese	1 tbsp

Preheat the oven to 180°C (350°F or Mark 4). Lightly grease four 20 cl (7 fl oz) soufflé dishes and place them on a baking sheet.

Cook the artichokes in a saucepan of boiling water for 6 to 8 minutes, or until they are tender. Drain and mash them, and set them aside.

In a large, heavy-bottomed saucepan, blend the cornflour with a little of the milk. Stir in the remaining milk, followed by the mace, salt, parsley and some black pepper. Bring to the boil, stirring continuously, then reduce the heat to medium and cook the sauce for about 2 minutes, until thickened. Remove the pan from the heat and stir in the mashed artichokes. Set aside 1 tablespoon of the walnuts, stir the

remainder into the pan, together with the egg yolk, and mix the ingredients well.

Whisk the egg whites until stiff then, using a metal tablespoon, carefully fold a quarter of the whites at a time into the artichoke mixture. Divide the mixture equally among the prepared dishes. Sprinkle the top of the soufflés with the Parmesan and reserved walnuts, and bake them in the oven for 20 to 25 minutes, or until they are well risen and golden. Remove the soufflés from the oven and serve them immediately.

Suggested accompaniment: crusty wholemeal bread; green salad with a garlic dressing.

Lentil Soufflés Baked in Sweet Pepper Cases

Serves 6

Working time: about 40 minutes

Total time: about 2 hours

Calories 165
Protein 10g
Cholesterol 75mg
Total fat 5g
Saturated fat 1g
Sodium 130mg

1 tbsp	virgin olive oil	1 tbsp
1	large onion, finely chopped	1
1	large carrot, finely chopped	1
1	garlic clove, crushed	1
175 g	split red lentils, picked over, rinsed	6 oz

45 cl	unsalted vegetable stock	¾ pint
¼ tsp	salt	¼ tsp
	freshly ground black pepper	
2 tbsp	tomato paste	2 tbsp
3	large sweet green peppers	3
2	eggs, separated	2

Heat the oil in a large, heavy-bottomed saucepan over medium heat. Add the onion and carrot and cook gently for 5 minutes. Stir in the garlic, lentils, stock, salt and tomato paste. Bring the mixture to the boil, then reduce the heat, cover the pan tightly and simmer for 45 minutes, until the lentils are soft and the stock has been absorbed.

Meanwhile, carefully remove the stalk from each pepper. Cut the peppers in half horizontally and remove their seeds and any thick white ribs. Cook the pepper cups in gently simmering water to cover for 4 to 5 minutes until softened, then drain them well on paper towels. Place the cups in a lightly oiled, shallow ovenproof dish. Preheat the oven to 190°C (375°F or Mark 5).

Remove the cooked lentils from the heat and allow them to cool for 10 minutes. Season with some pepper, then beat in the egg yolks. Whisk the egg whites until stiff but not dry; fold 1 tablespoon into the lentil mixture to lighten it, then fold in the remainder. Spoon the soufflé mixture into the pepper cups and cook for 30 to 35 minutes, until the soufflés are well risen and lightly browned. Serve immediately.

Suggested accompaniments: tomato salad; crusty bread.

Soufflé of Smoked Trout

Serves 6

Working time: about 30 minutes

Total time: about 1 hour and 20 minutes

Calories 225

Protein 24g

Cholesterol 145mg

Total fat 9g

Saturated fat 3g

Sodium 305mg

1	small smoked trout fillet, skinned and boned, the flesh shredded (about 60 g/2 oz)	1
4	freshwater trout, filleted (about 500 g/1 lb of fillets) or 500 g (1 lb) sea trout fillets	4
2 tbsp	finely cut fresh dill	2 tbsp
2 tbsp	fresh lemon juice	2 tbsp
15 g	unsalted butter	½ oz
1	onion, finely chopped	1
6 tbsp	plain flour	6 tbsp
¼ litre	skimmed milk	8 fl oz
¼ litre	fish stock, or an additional ¼ litre (8 fl oz) skimmed milk	8 fl oz
¼ tsp	fresh thyme, or ⅛ tsp dried thyme	¼ tsp
⅛ tsp	grated nutmeg	⅛ tsp
¼ tsp	salt	¼ tsp
	freshly ground black pepper	
2	egg yolks	2
8	egg whites	8
⅛ tsp	cream of tartar	⅛ tsp

Preheat the oven to 220°C (425°F or Mark 7). Rinse the trout fillets and pat dry with paper towels. Wrap fillets in a single piece of aluminium foil, its dull side out, and put on a baking sheet. Bake until they are opaque – approximately 15 minutes.

Unwrap fillets and allow to cool. Flake the flesh, carefully picking out all the bones. In a large bowl, combine the fresh trout with the smoked trout, the dill and the lemon juice. Set aside.

Fry onion in melted butter for about 4 minutes. Meanwhile, put flour in a bowl and stir in milk and the stock. Pour this mixture into the onion pan and

bring to the boil, whisking constantly. Remove from heat and whisk in the thyme, nutmeg, salt, pepper and egg yolks; set aside and keep warm.

Beat egg whites in a bowl with the cream of tartar until stiff. Stir the milk-and-stock mixture into fish mixture. Stir one quarter of egg whites into fish mixture; gently fold in the remaining whites.

Pour into a buttered 2 litre (3½ pint) soufflé dish and put in the oven. Immediately reduce the oven temperature to 190°C (375°F or Mark 5) and bake until soufflé is golden and set – about 45 minutes. Serve.

Fennel and Lentil Pâté

Serves 10 as a first course

Working time: about 50 minutes

Total time: 5 hours

Calories 100
Protein 9g
Cholesterol 0mg
Total fat 1g
Saturated fat trace
Sodium 225mg

250 g	green lentils, picked over and rinsed	8 oz
1	large onion, chopped	1
2	garlic cloves, crushed	2
250 g	bulb fennel, trimmed and chopped, feathery tops reserved and chopped	8 oz
1 tsp	safflower oil	1 tsp
4 tbsp	plain low-fat yogurt	4 tbsp
1 tsp	mild chili powder	1 tsp
2 tsp	fresh lemon juice	2 tsp
1 tsp	salt	1 tsp
3 tbsp	chopped parsley	3 tbsp
	freshly ground black pepper	
1 tsp	dry mustard	1 tsp
4 tsp	powdered gelatine	4 tsp
4	egg whites	4
	lime slices, for garnish	
	fennel tops, for garnish	

Boil lentils in a saucepan with plenty of water. Add half of the onion and garlic, cover and reduce heat. Simmer for 40 minutes, until tender. Leave to drain in a sieve.

Meanwhile, bring the bulb fennel to boil in another pan. Simmer for about 15 minutes, or until it is tender. Drain, reserving 2 tablespoons of the cooking liquid and leave to cool.

Sauté remaining onion and garlic in safflower oil – about 5 minutes.

Purée the drained lentils and turn the purée into a bowl. Add yogurt, chili, fennel tops, half of lemon juice and salt, 2 tablespoons of the parsley and a generous grinding of pepper. Mix together well.

Purée fennel and the sautéed onion and garlic until smooth. Transfer to bowl; mix in mustard, remaining salt and lemon juice, and some black pepper.

Dissolve gelatine in reserved fennel-cooking water. Thoroughly mix ½ of the gelatine solution into the lentil mixture and the other ½ into the fennel purée.

Whisk the egg whites until stiff. Divide whites between bowls and fold in. Sprinkle parsley over base of a 1 lb (500 g) loaf tin lined with greaseproof paper and fill with a layer of fennel sandwiched between 2 layers of lentil mix, chilling for 10 minutes between each. Chill for 3 hours. Serve garnished and sliced as illustration.

Iced Apple Mousse Cake with Brandy Snaps

Serves 12

Working time: about 1 hour

Total time: 2½ to 4 hours, depending on freezing method

Calories 175
Protein 2g
Cholesterol 10mg
Total fat 4g
Saturated fat 2g
Sodium 30mg

1 kg	crisp eating apples	**2 lb**	**6**	egg whites	**6**
4 tbsp	fresh lemon juice	**4 tbsp**	**12**	tuile brandy snaps	**12**
½ tsp	ground cloves	**½ tsp**			
½ tsp	ground cinnamon	**½ tsp**		**Apple Fans**	
30 g	unsalted butter	**1 oz**	**2**	crisp eating apples	**2**
100 g	caster sugar	**3½ oz**	**2 tsp**	honey	**2 tsp**

To make the apple mousse, peel and core the 1 kg (2 lb) of apples, then cut them into 1 cm (½ inch) chunks. Toss the apples with the lemon juice, cloves and cinnamon.

Melt the butter in a large, heavy frying pan over medium heat. Add the apple mixture and cook it, stirring frequently, for about 10 minutes. Sprinkle in the sugar and continue to cook the mixture stirring often, for 5 minutes.

Put the apple mixture into a food processor or a blender and process it until it is very smooth, stopping at least once to scrape down the sides. Transfer the mixture to a shallow bowl and whisk in the egg whites. Freeze the mixture.

Preheat the oven to 180°C (350°F or Mark 4).

To prepare the apple fans, peel the remaining two apples and cut them in half lengthwise.

Remove the cores, then slice the apple halves thinly, keeping the slices together. Fan out each sliced apple half on a baking sheet. Dribble the honey over the fans and bake them until they are tender – about 15 minutes. Allow the fans to cool to room temperature, then refrigerate them.

Transfer the apple mousse to a 23 cm (9 inch) spring-form tin and freeze it until it is solid – about 1 hour.

To unmould the cake, run a knife round the inside of the tin, then place a hot, damp towel on the bottom for about 10 seconds. Invert a plate on the cake; turn both cake and plate over together. Remove the sides of the tin, and smooth the surface with a long knife or spatula.

Arrange the chilled apple fans on top of the cake with the brandy snaps.

Frozen Lemon Meringue Torte

Serves 8

Working
time: about
1 hour and
15 minutes

Total time:
1½ to
4 hours

Calories
240
Protein
4g
Cholesterol
0mg
Total fat
5g
Saturated fat
0g
Sodium
30mg

8	lemons	8		**Almond Meringues**	
250 g	caster sugar	8 oz	2	egg whites	2
2	egg whites	2	6 tbsp	cocoa powder	6 tbsp
2 tbsp	cocoa powder	2 tbsp	75 g	blanched almonds, ground	2¼ oz
			2 tbsp	icing sugar	2 tbsp

Grate the rind from three of the lemons and put it into a food processor. Working over a bowl to catch the juice, peel and segment one of the lemons. Squeeze the pulpy core of membranes to extract every bit of juice. Repeat the process with the remaining lemons. To remove seeds, strain the juice into the food processor. Add the segments, sugar, 2 egg whites and 55 cl (18 fl oz) of water to the rind and juice, and purée.

Freeze the lemon mixture.

Preheat the oven to 110°C (200°F or Mark¼). Line a baking sheet with greaseproof paper.

Beat the two egg whites until they form soft peaks, adding sugar a tablespoon at a time; when all sugar has been incorporated, continue beating until glossy and stiff. Fold the almonds in.

Pipe the meringue on to the prepared baking sheet in strips nearly the length of the sheet; about 2.5 cm (1 inch) wide and 2.5 cm (1 inch) apart. Sprinkle the strips with the icing sugar, then bake for 1 hour.

Turn off oven and let strips dry, with oven door ajar, for another hour. Remove the baking sheet from oven and gently loosen meringues. Break the meringues into bars about 7.5 cm (3 inches) long; when cooled, store in an airtight container until ready for use.

When the sorbet is frozen, transfer it to a 20 or 23 cm (8 or 9 inch) springform tin. Distribute the sorbet evenly in the tin. Freeze for 1 hour.

Ease the torte onto a serving plate and press meringue bars into a pattern on top and sides. Serve dusted with cocoa powder.

Amaretto Custards with Plum Sauce

Serves 6

Working time: about 30 minutes

Total time: about 1 hour and 30 minutes

Calories 250
Protein 8g
Cholesterol 100mg
Total fat 7g
Saturated fat 2g
Sodium 95mg

25 g	almonds, sliced	**¾ oz**
1¼ tsp	ground cinnamon	**1¼ tsp**
5 tbsp	caster sugar	**5 tbsp**
2	eggs, plus 2 egg whites	**2**
4 tbsp	amaretto liqueur	**4 tbsp**
90 g	honey	**3 oz**
55 cl	semi-skimmed milk	**18 fl oz**
4	ripe red plums, quartered and stoned	**4**
2 tsp	fresh lemon juice	**2 tsp**

Preheat the oven to 170°C (325°F or Mark 3). Toast the almonds in the oven as it preheats until they are golden – about 25 minutes.

Lightly butter six 12.5 cl (4 fl oz) ramekins. In a small dish, mix ¾ teaspoon of the cinnamon with 2 tablespoons of the sugar. Put about 1 teaspoon of the cinnamon-and-sugar mixture into each ramekin, then tilt it to coat its buttered sides and bottom. Put the ramekins into a large, ovenproof baking dish and refrigerate.

In a large bowl, whisk together the eggs, egg whites, amaretto, honey and the remaining ½ teaspoon of cinnamon. Whisk in the milk, then pour the mixture into the ramekins, filling each to within 5 mm (¼ inch) of the top.

Place the baking dish with the filled ramekins in the oven. Pour hot tap water into the baking

dish two thirds of the way up the sides of the ramekins. Bake the custards until a knife inserted in the centre of one comes out clean – about 30 minutes. Remove the ramekins from the dish and let them cool for half an hour.

While custards cool, prepare the plum sauce. Purée plums, remaining 3 tablespoons of sugar and lemon juice until smooth. Sieve into a bowl to remove skins. Refrigerate until chilled – about half an hour.

Run a small, sharp knife round the inside of each ramekin. Invert a serving plate over the top and turn both over together. Lift away the ramekin. Ladle some of the plum sauce round each custard; sprinkle the toasted almonds over the top.

Lemon-Buttermilk Custards with Candied Lemon

Serves 8

Working
time: about
20 minutes

Total time:
about
2 hours and
40 minutes
(includes
chilling)

Calories
185
Protein
5g
Cholesterol
70mg
Total fat
2g
Saturated fat
1g
Sodium
115mg

2	eggs	2
200 g	caster sugar	7 oz
45 g	plain flour	1½ oz
2 tsp	pure lemon extract	2 tsp

¾ litre	buttermilk	1¼ pints
3	lemons, thinly sliced, for garnish	3
60 g	raspberries for garnish	2 oz

Preheat the oven to 150°C (300°F or Mark 2).

To prepare the custard, first whisk the eggs in a bowl, then whisk in 135 g (4½ oz) of the sugar and the flour; when the custard is smooth, stir in the lemon extract and buttermilk. Pour the custard into eight 12.5 cl (4 fl oz) ramekins and set them on a baking sheet. Bake the custards until they are puffed up and set, and a knife inserted at the edge comes out clean – 15 to 20 minutes. Let the custards cool slightly, then refrigerate them until they are well chilled – about 2 hours.

To make the candied lemon slices, lightly oil a baking sheet and set it aside. Combine the remaining sugar with 4 tablespoons of water in a small, heavy-bottomed saucepan. Bring the mixture to the boil, then reduce the heat to low and cook, stirring occasionally, until the sugar has dissolved and the syrup is clear – about 1½ minutes. Add the lemon slices to the pan; immediately turn the slices over, coating them well, and cook them for about 30 seconds. Transfer the slices to the oiled baking sheet.

To serve, run a small knife round the inside of each ramekin and invert the custards on to serving plates. Garnish each plate with a few candied lemon slices and a sprinkle of fresh raspberries.

Maple Mousse with Glazed Apple Nuggets

Serves 6

Working time: about 1 hour

Total time: about 1 hour and 45 minutes

Calories
215
Protein
2g
Cholesterol
25mg
Total fat
7g
Saturated fat
4g
Sodium
35mg

15 g	unsalted butter	**½ oz**
2	tart green apples, peeled, cored and cut into 1 cm (½ inch) cubes	**2**
1 tsp	fresh lemon juice	**1 tsp**
175 g	maple syrup	**6 oz**
6 tbsp	double cream	**6 tbsp**
½ tsp	pure vanilla extract	**½ tsp**
3	egg whites, at room temperature	**3**
5 tbsp	light brown sugar	**5 tbsp**

Melt the butter in a frying pan set over medium-high heat. When the butter is hot, add the apple cubes and lemon juice; sauté the cubes, until they are light brown – about 10 minutes. Dribble 1 tablespoon of the maple syrup over the cubes and sauté them for 1 minute more. Transfer the glazed apple cubes to a plate and refrigerate them.

Whip the cream until it holds stiff peaks, stir in vanilla, then refrigerate. Put egg whites into a deep bowl and set aside.

Combine half of the remaining maple syrup and the sugar in a small pan. Bring to the boil and cook it to the soft-ball stage over medium heat. Begin testing after 4 minutes: drop a bit of the syrup into a bowl filled with iced water. When the mixture forms a ball, start beating the egg whites with an electric mixer on medium-high speed. Pour the hot syrup into the whites in a thin, steady stream, beating as you pour. Continue to beat the whites until meringue has cooled to room temperature – about 7 minutes. Fold the cream and apple into the meringue. (Do not overfold.) Immediately spoon into six individual dishes and refrigerate for at least 45 minutes.

Bring the remaining syrup to the boil in a small pan. Cook over medium heat, stirring frequently, until the mixture crystallizes – about 15 minutes. Allow the mixture to cool for 10 minutes, stirring occasionally. Scrape the crystallized sugar out of the pan to a clean work surface. Using a rolling pin, crush the sugar until it is finely crumbled.

Just before serving, sprinkle some of the maple sugar on to each portion of mousse.

Orange and Buttermilk Parfaits

<table>
<tr><td>Serves 8</td></tr>
<tr><td>Working time: about 40 minutes</td></tr>
<tr><td>Total time: about 1 hour and 10 minutes</td></tr>
</table>

Calories
145

Protein
5g

Cholesterol
70mg

Total fat
2g

Saturated fat
1g

Sodium
75mg

35 cl	buttermilk	**12 fl oz**
½ tbsp	powdered gelatine	**½ tbsp**
150 g	sugar	**5 oz**
2	eggs, separated, plus 1 egg white	**2**
4 tbsp	frozen orange juice concentrate, thawed	**4 tbsp**
2	oranges, for garnish	**2**

Put ¼ litre (8 fl oz) of the buttermilk, the gelatine, 4 tablespoons of the sugar and the egg yolks into a small saucepan over low heat. Cook the mixture, stirring constantly, until it coats the back of the spoon – 6 to 8 minutes. (Do not let the mixture come to the boil or it will curdle.) Divide between two bowls; whisk remaining buttermilk into one; whisk orange juice into the other. Set both aside at room temperature.

Pour the egg whites into a deep bowl. Then set up an electric mixer; you will need to start beating the egg whites as soon as the syrup is ready.

Heat the remaining sugar with 4 tablespoons of water in a small saucepan over medium-high heat. Boil until the bubbles rise to the surface in a random pattern, indicating that the water has nearly evaporated and the sugar itself is beginning to cook. With a small spoon, drop a little of the syrup into a bowl filled with iced water. If the syrup dissolves immediately, continue cooking. When syrup dropped into water can be rolled between your fingers into a ball, start the mixer.

Beat the egg whites at high speed. Pour the syrup into the bowl in a very thin, steady stream. Decrease the speed to medium; continue beating until the egg whites are glossy, formed stiff peaks and cooled to room temperature. Increase speed to high and beat the meringue for 1 minute more.

Mix a few heaped spoonfuls of the meringue into each of the buttermilk mixtures. Fold half of the remaining meringue into each mixture.

Spoon mixture containing extra buttermilk into eight glasses and top with the orange mixture. Refrigerate parfaits for 30 minutes.

Segment the two oranges and use to garnish each portion.

Mile-High Pie with Two Sauces

Serves 12

Working time: about 1 hour

Total time: about 2 hours

Calories 240
Protein 6g
Cholesterol 70mg
Total fat 3g
Saturated fat 1g
Sodium 85mg

1 tbsp	safflower oil	1 tbsp
315 g	caster sugar	10½ oz
12	egg whites	12
1 tbsp	pure vanilla extract	1 tbsp
¼ tsp	cream of tartar	¼ tsp
	Vanilla-Yogurt Sauce	
30 cl	semi-skimmed milk	½ pint
1	vanilla pod	1
3	egg yolks	3

2 tbsp	caster sugar	2 tbsp
¼ litre	plain low-fat yogurt	8 fl oz
	Cranberry Sauce	
200 g	fresh or frozen cranberries, picked over	7 oz
100 g	caster sugar	3½ oz
12.5 cl	ruby port	4 fl oz
6 tbsp	plain low-fat yogurt	6 tbsp

Oil a 23 cm (9 inch) springform tin and sprinkle in 15 g (½ oz) of the sugar; tilt pan to cover with the sugar. Preheat the oven to 150°C (300°F or Mark 2).

Put egg whites, vanilla extract and cream of tartar into a bowl and beat at low speed gradually increasing speed to medium as the whites turn opaque. Add remaining sugar a tablespoon at a time, increasing the speed all the while. Continue beating on high speed until glossy and when beater is, lifted stiff peaks form.

Transfer meringue to tin. Smooth top of meringue and bake the pie until risen and lightly browned – about 40 minutes. It will be moist throughout. Remove pie from the oven and let it cool to room temperature in the tin.

Heat the milk, vanilla pod, egg yolks and sugar in a small heavy-bottomed, saucepan set over low heat. Cook, stirring constantly, until thick enough to coat the back of the spoon. Strain into a bowl; when it has cooled to room temperature, whisk in the yogurt.

Cook the cranberries, sugar and 12.5 cl (4 fl oz) of water in a pan over medium-high heat until they have burst and are quite soft – about 12 minutes. Sieve into a bowl, cool to room temperature; whisk in port and yogurt.

To serve, remove sides of tin and present with the sauces, perhaps swirled as in illustration.

Spiced Pumpkin Mousse with Lemon Cream

Serves 6

Working time: about 30 minutes

Total time: about 2 hours (includes chilling)

Calories 140
Protein 4g
Cholesterol 18mg
Total fat 5g
Saturated fat 3g
Sodium 90mg

2½ tsp	powdered gelatine	**2½ tsp**
6 tbsp	caster sugar	**6 tbsp**
2 tsp	grated lemon rind	**2 tsp**
¾ tsp	aniseeds, finely ground	**¾ tsp**
⅛ tsp	grated nutmeg	**⅛ tsp**
1 tbsp	finely chopped crystallized ginger	**1 tbsp**
⅛ tsp	salt	**⅛ tsp**
250 g	canned pumpkin	**8 oz**
4 tbsp	fresh lemon juice	**4 tbsp**
4	egg whites, at room temperature	**4**
⅛ tsp	cream of tartar	**⅛ tsp**

Lemon Cream

25 g	lemon rind, julienned	**¾ oz**
2 tbsp	caster sugar	**2 tbsp**
2 tbsp	fresh lemon juice	**2 tbsp**
6 tbsp	double cream	**6 tbsp**

Put 4 tablespoons of cold water into a bowl, then sprinkle in the gelatine. Let the gelatine soften for 5 minutes; pour in 4 tablespoons of boiling water and stir to dissolve. Stir in the sugar, lemon rind, ground aniseeds, nutmeg, ginger and salt. Add the pųmpkin and lemon juice, and stir. Chill the mixture in the refrigerator, stirring occasionally, until it starts to gel – about 30 minutes.

Beat egg whites with cream of tartar in a bow'l until they form stiff peaks. Remove pumpkin mixture from refrigerator and whisk vigorously. Stir in one third of the egg whites and combine thoroughly, then fold in remaining egg whites.

Divide mousse into six portions and chill for 1 to 6 hours.

Put the lemon rind in a small, pan with 4 tablespoons of water, the 2 tablespoons of sugar and the 2 tablespoons of lemon juice. Bring to the boil, then reduce the heat, and simmer the mixture until it becomes a thick syrup – about 5 minutes. Strain into a small bowl, reserving the rind. Set half of the cooked rind aside; finely chop the rest.

Just before serving, whip the cream in a small bowl. Fold in syrup and the grated lemon rind. Garnish each with the lemon cream and a few strands of the reserved rind.

Greek Yogurt Flan

Serves 8		Calories 115
Working time: about 40 minutes		Protein 3g
		Cholesterol 60mg
Total time: about 3 hours (includes chilling)		Total fat 3g
		Saturated fat 1g
		Sodium 40mg

2	eggs	**2**
1	egg white	**1**
90 g	caster sugar	**3 oz**
90 g	plain flour	**3 oz**
250 g	thick Greek yogurt	**8 oz**
1 tbsp	sifted icing sugar	**1 tbsp**

1	orange, finely grated rind only	**1**
3 tbsp	orange juice mixed with 3 tbsp cointreau	**3 tbsp**
8	fresh ripe figs, each cut into 8 pieces, skin removed if bitter	**8**

Heat the oven to 180°C (350°F or Mark 4). Butter a 22 cm (10 inch) fluted sponge flan tin. Put the eggs, egg white and sugar into a large bowl and beat with an electric mixer for 6 – 8 minutes. Sift the flour on top of this mixture and fold in. Pour the mixture into the prepared tin and spread it evenly. Bake for 25 minutes, until very lightly browned and springy to the touch. Turn out on to a wire rack to cool.

Put one third of the yogurt into a piping bag fitted with a star nozzle and refrigerate until needed. Mix the remaining yogurt with the icing sugar and the finely grated orange rind.

Place the sponge flan on a serving dish. Spoon the orange juice and cointreau evenly over the centre of the flan, then spread the orange-flavoured yogurt on top. Pipe a decorative border round the edge with the yogurt in the piping bag. Arrange the fig pieces on the yogurt in the centre. Cover loosely with plastic film and chill in the refrigerator for 1 hour before serving.

Strawberry Trifle Gateau

Serves 8

Working time: about 35 minutes

Total time: about 6 hours (includes chilling)

Calories 240

Protein 10g

Cholesterol 90mg

Total fat 3g

Saturated fat 1g

Sodium 50mg

3	eggs	**3**	**125 g**	plain flour	**4 oz**
1	egg white	**1**	**250 g**	quark	**8 oz**
200 g	caster sugar	**7 oz**	**1 tsp**	pure vanilla extract	**1 tsp**
750 g	fresh strawberries 500 g (1 lb) hulled and thinly sliced, the rest reserved for decoration	**1½ lb**	**1 tsp**	icing sugar	**1 tsp**
			15 g	shelled pistachio nuts, skinned and thinly sliced	**½ oz**

Heat the oven to 180°C (350°F or Mark 4). Lightly oil a 22 cm (10 inch) springform tin or cake tin. Line the base with greaseproof paper.

Put the whole eggs and egg white into a large bowl with 125 g (4 oz) of the caster sugar and prepare the sponge mixture as on page 49. Pour the mixture into the tin and spread it evenly. Bake for 25 to 30 minutes, until very lightly browned and springy to the touch. After a few minutes, then turn it out on to a wire rack to cool completely.

Meanwhile, put the sliced strawberries into a bowl with 50 g (2 oz) of the caster sugar. Mix well and leave to stand for about 1½ hours, to soften strawberries and draw out the juice. Blend the quark with the remaining sugar and vanilla.

Cut the cooled sponge in half horizontally. Place the bottom layer on a flat plate. Fit an expanding ring snugly round it (or, alternatively, a deep band of double thickness foil) in order to retain the shape. Spoon half the sliced strawberries and their juice over the sponge layer, then spread on the quark with the remaining sliced strawberries on top. Place the second sponge layer on top and cover with cling film and a plate. Place something heavy on top of the plate to weight down the gateau. Refrigerate for at least 4 hours.

To serve, remove the weight, plate and cling film. Carefully remove the ring. Slice the reserved strawberries for decoration. Sift on the icing sugar and sprinkle with the sliced pistachios. Refrigerate until ready to serve.

Berry-Filled Meringue Baskets

Serves 8	
Working time: about 50 minutes	
Total time: about 5 hours (includes drying)	

Calories 150	
Protein 4g	
Cholesterol 5mg	
Total fat 2g	
Saturated fat 1g	
Sodium 45mg	

3	egg whites	**3**
200 g	caster sugar	**7 oz**
125 g	low-fat ricotta cheese	**4 oz**
4 tbsp	plain low-fat yogurt	**4 tbsp**

350 g	hulled, sliced strawberries	**12 oz**
150 g	blueberries, stemmed, picked over and rinsed	**5 oz**

Line a baking sheet with non-stick parchment paper or brown paper. Preheat the oven to 70°C (160°F or Mark ¼). Keep the oven door propped open with a ball of crumpled foil.

To prepare the meringue, put the egg whites and sugar into a large, heatproof bowl. Set the bowl over a pan of simmering water, and stir the mixture with a whisk until the sugar has dissolved and the egg whites are hot – about 6 minutes. Remove the bowl from the heat. Using an electric mixer, beat the egg whites on medium-high speed until they form stiff peaks and have cooled to room temperature.

Transfer the meringue to a piping bag fitted with a 1 cm (½ inch) nozzle. Holding the nozzle about 1 cm (½ inch) above the surface of the

baking sheet, pipe out the meringue in a tightly coiled spiral until you have formed a flat disc about 8.5 cm (3½ inches) across. Pipe a single ring of meringue on top of the edge of the disc, forming a low wall that will hold in the filling. Form seven more meringue baskets in the same way.

Put the baking sheet into the oven and let the meringues bake for at least 4 hours. The meringues should remain white and be thoroughly dried out. Let the meringues stand at room temperature until they cool – they will become quite crisp.

Purée the ricotta with the yogurt in a food processor or a blender. Divide the cheese mixture among the meringue baskets, and top each with some of the strawberries and blueberries.

Cranberry Meringue Tartlets

Makes 18 tartlets				**Calories 115**		
Working time: about 1 hour				**Protein 2g**		
Total time: about 2 hours				**Cholesterol 0mg**		
				Total fat 4g		
				Saturated fat 1g		
				Sodium 50mg		

275 g	shortcrust dough	**9 oz**		**30 g**	caster sugar	**1 oz**
	Fruit Filling			**½ tsp**	arrowroot	**½ tsp**
175 g	fresh cranberries, picked over,	**6 oz**			**Meringue Topping**	
	or frozen cranberries, thawed			**2**	egg whites	**2**
3 tbsp	fresh orange juice	**3 tbsp**		**125 g**	caster sugar	**4 oz**
2 tbsp	clear honey	**2 tbsp**				

On a lightly floured surface, roll out the dough to a thickness of 3 mm (⅛ inch). Using a 7.5 cm (3 inch) cutter, stamp out 18 rounds and use these to line 6 cm (22 inch) tartlet tins. Prick the insides with a fork, then chill the tartlet cases for 30 minutes. Meanwhile, preheat the oven to 220°C (425°F or Mark 7).

Stand the tins on a baking sheet and bake the pastry cases for 15 to 20 minutes, until they are lightly browned and crisp. Remove from the oven, allow the cases to cool in the tins slightly, then unmould them on to a baking sheet. Reduce the oven temperature to 150°C (300°F or Mark 2).

Put the cranberries into a small pan with the orange juice and cook gently, covered, for about 8 minutes, until the fruit is soft and all the berries

have 'popped'. Stir in the honey and sugar, then add the arrowroot blended with 2 teaspoons of cold water. Bring the mixture back to the boil, stirring until it has thickened, then remove the pan from the heat and allow the filling to cool. Spoon the cooled cranberry mixture into the pastry cases.

To make the topping, whisk the egg whites until they form peaks, then whisk in the sugar, a tablespoon at a time, until the meringue is stiff and glossy. Transfer the meringue to a piping bag fitted with a 1 cm (½ inch) star nozzle and pipe a whirl on top of each tart to completely cover the filling. Return the tartlets to the oven and bake them for about 10 minutes, until the meringue is lightly tinged a pale brown.

Cornets Filled with Fruit Cream

Makes 30 cornets

Working time: about 50 minutes

Total time: about 1 hour and 20 minutes

Calories
50

Protein
1g

Cholesterol
15mg

Total fat
2g

Saturated fat
1g

Sodium
15mg

2	egg whites	**2**
60 g	caster sugar	**2 oz**
60 g	plain flour	**2 oz**
60 g	unsalted butter, melted and cooled	**2 oz**
60 g	mixed candied peel, finely chopped	**2 oz**
30 cl	pastry cream (see page 7)	**½ pint**

Preheat the oven to 190°C (375°F or Mark 5). Line two large baking sheets with non-stick parchment paper.

To make the cornets, first whisk the egg whites in a mixing bowl until they are frothy. Sprinkle the sugar over the surface and whisk for 2 to 3 minutes, until thick and shiny. Sift the flour over the surface, then fold it in very gently with the melted butter. Drop 2 to 3 teaspoons of mixture, spaced well apart, on to one of the baking sheets. Spread each spoonful out with the back of a spoon to form a circle 6 to 7.5 cm (2½ to 3 inches) in diameter. Bake for about 5 minutes, or until the edges are a light golden-brown. Meanwhile, make two or three more circles on the second sheet.

Remove the baked circles from the oven, and insert the second baking sheet. Quickly but carefully remove each of the baked circles in turn with a metal spatula, and mould it round a metal cream horn mould until set in shape. If the circles start to harden before they are all shaped, return them to the oven for a minute or so to soften them. Transfer the cornets to a wire rack to cool completely. Bake and shape the remaining mixture in the same way.

Just before serving, fold three quarters of the mixed candied peel into the pastry cream and spoon it into the sponge cornets. Decorate the filling with the remaining peel and serve.

Chocolate Mousse Layered Sponge

Makes 20 slices	
Working time: about 45 minutes	
Total time: about 1 hour and 25 minutes	

Calories 90	
Protein 3g	
Cholesterol 35mg	
Total fat 3g	
Saturated fat 1g	
Sodium 40mg	

3	egg yolks	**3**
100 g	vanilla-flavoured sugar	**3½ oz**
4	egg whites	**4**
125 g	plain flour	**4 oz**

Chocolate Mousse Filling		
½ tsp	powdered gelatine	**½ tsp**
100 g	plain chocolate, chopped	**3½ oz**
100 g	low-fat ricotta cheese, sieved	**3½ oz**
2	egg whites	**2**

Preheat the oven to 180°C (350°F or Mark 4). Grease a 25 by 18 cm (10 by 7 inch) baking tin and line the base with parchment paper.

To make sponge, put egg yolks and three quarters of sugar into a mixing bowl. Place bowl over a pan of hot, but not boiling, water set over a low heat. Whisk eggs and sugar together until thick and very pale. Remove bowl from pan and continue whisking until mixture is cool and falls from the whisk in a ribbon trail. Clean whisk and beat egg whites until stiff; sprinkle on the remaining sugar and whisk again until mixture becomes glossy. Sift a third of the flour over the surface of egg yolk mixture, add a third of the whites, gently but quickly fold in. Add remaining flour and whites in two more batches, using same technique.

Pour batter into tin and bake for 25 to 30 minutes, until sponge is well risen and springy to the touch.

Carefully unmould sponge on to a wire rack covered with greaseproof paper. Allow to cool for 2 to 3 minutes, then gently loosen the lining paper, but do not remove. Gently turn sponge right way up and leave to cool.

Sprinkle the gelatine over 1½ tablespoons of water in a small bowl. Leave it to soften for 2 minutes, then place the bowl over a pan of simmering water and stir until completely dissolved. Melt the chocolate in a large bowl placed over a pan of hot, not boiling, water. Remove the bowl from the heat and gradually beat in the ricotta straight away, keeping the mixture smooth. Beat in the gelatine; whisk egg whites until stiff then fold them into the mixture. Leave to set.

Cut cake in half lengthwise, then again horizontally and into 4 rectangles. Sandwich with 3 layers of mousse and cut into slices as illustration.

Chocolate-Orange Roulades

Makes 16
roulades

Working
time: about
1 hour

Total time:
about
1 hour and
30 minutes

Calories
195

Protein
4g

Cholesterol
60mg

Total fat
8g

Saturated fat
5g

Sodium
25mg

300 g	plain chocolate	**10 oz**		**1**	chocolate genoese sponge (see	**1**
1	egg yolk	**1**			page 8)	
1 tsp	Grand Marnier, Cointreau or	**1 tsp**		**15 g**	hazelnuts, toasted and skinned,	**½ oz**
	other orange-flavoured liqueur				chopped	
2	egg whites	**2**				

Melt 60 g (2 oz) of the chocolate in a heatproof bowl over a saucepan of simmering water. Allow it to cool slightly, then stir in the egg yolk and Grand Marnier. In a separate bowl, whisk the egg whites until they are very stiff, then fold them into the chocolate. Refrigerate the mousse until it has set – about 30 minutes.

Using a long serrated knife, cut the genoese sponge in half horizontally to make two thin sheets. Trim off any dry crusts. Cut each sheet in half lengthwise, then cut each strip crosswise into four, to give a total of sixteen 10 by 7.5 cm (4 by 3 inch) rectangles. Place each rectangle between two sheets of non-stick parchment paper and roll it a little with a rolling pin; this will flatten the sponge and prevent it from cracking

when it is rolled up with the filling.

Spread the cut surface of each rectangle with an even layer of chocolate mousse about 5 mm (¼ inch) thick; do not spread the mousse right up to the edges of the sponge. Working from a short edge, roll up each rectangle into a small tight roll.

Melt the remaining chocolate in a bowl over hot water. Place a roulade, seam-side down, on a metal spatula. Hold it over the bowl and spoon the melted chocolate over the roulade. Place the coated roll on a sheet of non-stick parchment paper and sprinkle it with chopped hazelnuts. Coat the remaining roulades in the same way and allow them to set before serving. When cool they will lift easily from the parchment paper.

Coconut Meringue Fingers

<table>
<tr><td>Makes
about 36
fingers

Working
time: about
30 minutes

Total time:
about
1 hour and
30 minutes</td><td></td><td>Calories
25
Protein
trace
Cholesterol
0mg
Total fat
1g
Saturated fat
trace
Sodium
5mg</td></tr>
</table>

| 2 | egg whites | 2 | 60 g | desiccated coconut | 2 oz |
| **125 g** | vanilla-flavoured caster sugar | **4 oz** | | | |

Preheat the oven to 130°C (250°F or Mark ½). Line two baking sheets with non-stick parchment paper.

Put the egg whites and sugar in a large, heatproof bowl. Set the bowl over a pan of simmering water, taking care that the bottom of the bowl does not touch the water, and whisk with an electric hand-held mixer until the mixture forms soft peaks – about 5 minutes. Remove the bowl from the heat and continue whisking at high speed until the meringue is stiff and glossy.

Using a metal spoon, lightly fold in all but 2 tablespoons of the coconut. Spoon the mixture into a piping bag fitted with a 1 cm (½ inch) plain nozzle and pipe out straight lines about 10 cm (4 inches) long on the prepared baking sheets. Sprinkle the remaining coconut over the tops of the fingers, then bake the fingers until they are crisp and dry but still white on the outside – about 1 hour. The meringue will still be slightly moist in the centre. Carefully transfer the fingers to a wire rack to cool.

Editor's Note: These fingers may be stored in an airtight container for four to five days.

A Trio of Meringues

Makes 24
meringues

Working
time: about
1 hour

Total time:
about
4 hours

Per plain
meringue:

Calories
80
Protein
2g
Cholesterol
0mg
Total fat
2g
Saturated fat
1g
Sodium
60mg

4	egg whites	4
250 g	caster sugar	8 oz
45 g	desiccated coconut, lightly toasted	1½ oz
30 g	raspberries, puréed and sieved	1 oz
30 g	plain chocolate, finely grated	1 oz

30 g	shelled walnuts, finely chopped	1 oz
	Lemon-Cheese Filling	
250 g	low-fat curd cheese	8 oz
2	lemons, finely grated rind only	2
30 g	caster sugar	1 oz

Preheat oven to 100°C (200°F or Mark ¼). Line three baking sheets with parchment paper.

In large bowl, whisk egg whites until stiff but not dry. Gradually whisk in the caster sugar, a little at a time, whisking between each addition until the meringue is very stiff and shiny.

Put one third of meringue into a piping bag fitted with a 12-point 1 cm (½ inch) star nozzle. Mix another third of meringue in a bowl with 30 g (1 oz) of coconut, then spoon into a piping bag fitted with a 1.5 cm (⅝ inch) plain nozzle. Fold raspberry purée into the remaining meringue, then spoon it into a piping bag fitted with a seven-point 1 cm (½ inch) star nozzle.

Pipe each type of meringue mixture into different shapes as in illustrated suggestion.

Bake the meringues until they are crisp and dry: the coconut ones need about 2 hours, the others from 2½ to 3 hours, depending on size. If they begin to brown before they are crisp, lower or turn off the oven. Allow the meringues to cool on the baking sheets before removing them from the paper.

For the filling, beat the curd cheese in a bowl with the lemon rind and sugar until the mixture is smooth. Just before serving the meringues, sandwich them together in matching pairs with the lemon cheese. Sprinkle the plain meringues with the grated chocolate, the coconut meringues with the remaining 15 g (½ oz) of the toasted coconut, and the raspberry meringues with the chopped walnut.

Hazelnut Scallops with Chocolate Icing

3	egg whites	**3**	**1½ tsp**	strong black coffee, cooled	**1½ tsp**
175 g	caster sugar	**6 oz**	**7 g**	unsalted butter	**¼ oz**
90 g	shelled hazelnuts, toasted and skinned, ground	**3 oz**	**30 g**	icing sugar	**1 oz**
60 g	plain chocolate	**2 oz**	**1 tbsp**	frangelico or amaretto liqueur	**1 tbsp**

Preheat the oven to 100°C (200°F or Mark ¼). Line a large baking sheet with non-stick parchment paper.

Whisk the egg whites until they are very stiff. Beat in the sugar, a little at a time, whisking well between each addition until the meringue is stiff and glossy. Fold in the hazelnuts with a metal spoon.

Transfer the meringue to a piping bag fitted with a 2cm (¾ inch) star nozzle, and pipe 40 scallop shapes on to the lined baking sheet. bake for 2¼ hours, or until the meringues feel firm to the touch and come away from the paper

easily. Turn off the oven but leave the meringues inside until they are cold and completely dry – about 4 hours, or overnight.

Melt the chocolate with the coffee in a heatproof bowl set over a pan of simmering water. Stir in the butter. Sift in the icing sugar and beat well. Allow to cool briefly, then stir in the liqueur. Leave a few minutes more, until thickened slightly. Sandwich meringues in pairs with the icing, and dip the ends in the icing. Place the scallops on a sheet of non-stick parchment paper until the icing has set – about 1 hour.

Walnut Meringues with Rose-Water Cream

Makes 10 meringues

Working time: about 30 minutes

Total time: about 7 hours

Calories 155
Protein 2g
Cholesterol 15mg
Total fat 8g
Saturated fat 3g
Sodium 20mg

3	egg whites	3
175 g	caster sugar	6 oz
45 g	shelled walnuts, chopped and lightly toasted	1½ oz
15 cl	whipping cream	¼ pint
¼ tsp	rose-water	¼ tsp
350 g	strawberries, hulled and thinly sliced	12 oz

Preheat the oven to 100°C (200°F or Mark ¼). Line a baking sheet with non-stick parchment paper.

Whisk the egg whites until the mixture is so stiff that it clings to the whisk when it is held upside down. Add the caster sugar, a little at a time, whisking constantly after each addition until the mixture is again stiff and glossy. With a metal spoon, fold in the chopped walnuts and half of the rose-water.

Transfer the mixture to a piping bag fitted with a 2 cm (¾ inch) star nozzle, and pipe 20 small whirls about 5 cm (2 inches) in diameter on to the prepared baking sheet. Bake the meringues for 2½ hours until they can be lifted easily off the paper, then turn off the oven but leave the meringues inside until they are cold and completely dry – about 4 hours, or overnight.

Just before serving, whip the cream in a bowl, add the remaining ⅛ teaspoon of rose-water, and gently fold in the sliced strawberries. Sandwich pairs of meringues together with this filling.

Editor's Note: To toast walnuts, put them under a hot grill for about a minute, shaking frequently.

Pistachio Meringues

Makes 12 meringues

Working time: about 30 minutes

Total time: about 7 hours

Calories 135

Protein 2g

Cholesterol 15mg

Total fat 7g

Saturated fat 3g

Sodium 20mg

3	egg whites	**3**
60 g	shelled pistachio nuts, skinned, 15 g (½ oz) chopped, remainder cut into slivers	**2 oz**
175 g	caster sugar	**6 oz**
15 cl	whipping cream	**¼ pint**
1	kiwi fruit, peeled and sliced, slices quartered	**1**

Preheat the oven to 100°C (200°C or Mark ¼). Line two baking sheets with non-stick parchment paper.

Whisk the egg whites until the mixture is so stiff that it clings to the whisk when it is held upside down. Gradually add the sugar, a little at a time, whisking constantly after each addition until the mixture is again stiff and glossy. With a metal spoon, gently fold in the slivered pistachio nuts. Transfer the mixture to a piping bag fitted with a 2.5 cm (1 inch) plain nozzle and pipe 24 small meringues, each about 5 cm (2 inches) in diameter, on to the prepared baking sheets.

Bake the meringues for 2½ hours, until they will move easily on the paper. Turn off the oven and allow the meringues to rest in the oven until they are cold and completely dry – about 4 hours, or overnight.

Just before serving, whip the cream in a bowl and use it to sandwich the meringues together in pairs; for a decorative effect, pipe the cream through a star nozzle. Decorate the meringues with the chopped pistachio nuts and kiwi quarters. Serve immediately.

Editor's Note: To skin pistachio nuts, blanch them in boiling water for 1 minute, drain them and rub them briskly in a towel until they have shed their skins.

Cherry-Chocolate Meringue Nests

Makes 8 nests

Working time: about 45 minutes

Total time: about 6 hours

Calories 145
Protein 2g
Cholesterol 0mg
Total fat 3g
Saturated fat 2g
Sodium 15mg

2	egg whites	**2**
125 g	caster sugar	**4 oz**
45 g	plain chocolate	**1½ oz**
1 tbsp	kirsch	**1 tbsp**
150 g	fromage frais	**5 oz**
150 g	cherries, stoned and halved	**5 oz**
3 tbsp	cherry jam	**3 tbsp**
1 tsp	arrowroot	**1 tsp**

Preheat the oven to 100°C (200°F or Mark ¼). Line a baking sheet with non-stick parchment paper and pencil eight 7.5 by 5 cm (3 by 2 inch) ovals on to the paper; leave at least 2.5 cm (1 inch) between ovals. Turn the paper over so that the marks face downwards.

Put egg whites and sugar into a large bowl over a pan of simmering water, taking care that the bowl does not touch the water. Stir mixture with a whisk until sugar has dissolved and egg whites are hot – about 4 minutes – then whisk vigorously until the meringue is stiff and glossy.

Spoon the meringue into a piping bag fitted with a 1 cm (½ inch) star nozzle, and make bases by filling in the pencilled ovals on the baking paper with piped coils of meringue. To make the sides of the nests, pipe two layers – one on top of the other – round the edge of each base. Bake the nests until they are crisp and dry, but not brown – 5 to 6 hours. Carefully transfer them to a wire rack to cool.

Melt the chocolate in a heatproof bowl set over a pan of simmering water. Carefully paint the base inside each nest with a thin layer of melted chocolate.

Beat the kirsch into the *fromage frais* and, when the chocolate has set, spoon it into the nests. Top the flavoured *fromage frais* with the halved cherries.

In a small saucepan, heat the jam with 2 tablespoons of water until liquid. Sieve the melted jam to remove any solids, then stir in the arrowroot. Return the mixture to the pan and bring it to the boil, stirring constantly. Remove the pan from the heat and allow the glaze to thicken before brushing it carefully over the cherries in each nest.

Fruit-Filled Meringue Baskets

Makes 8 baskets

Working time: about 45 minutes

Total time: about 3 hours and 45 minutes

Calories 85
Protein 1g
Cholesterol 0mg
Total fat 0g
Saturated fat 0g
Sodium 15mg

90 g	caster sugar	**3 oz**	**1**	kiwi fruit, peeled, halved lengthwise and sliced	**1**
30 g	light brown sugar	**1 oz**	**60 g**	green seedless grapes, halved	**2 oz**
2	egg whites	**2**	**125 g**	fresh strawberries, hulled and sliced	**4 oz**
	Fruit Filling		**2 tbsp**	kirsch or dry white wine	**2 tbsp**
90 g	fresh raspberries	**3 oz**			

Heat the oven to 100°C (200°F or Mark ¼). Line a large baking sheet with non-stick parchment paper and pencil eight 6 cm (2½ inch) squares on the paper, spaced at least 2.5 cm (1 inch) apart. Turn the paper over so that the marks face downwards.

Sift together the caster sugar and brown sugar. Whisk the egg whites until they form soft peaks. Continue whisking while gradually adding the combined sugars, a tablespoon at a time; the mixture should be stiff and glossy after each addition of sugar. Transfer the meringue to a piping bag fitted with a 1 cm (½ inch) star nozzle. First pipe round the edge of each outlined square on the baking paper, then pipe back and forth across the squares to make bases for the baskets. Make sides for the baskets by piping a border, two layers high, round the edge of each base. Complete the baskets with a meringue 'star' at each corner.

Cook the meringues until they are completely dry and will lift easily off the paper – 2½ to 3 hours. Cool them on a wire rack.

Put the raspberries, kiwi slices, grape halves and strawberry slices in a bowl and stir in the kirsch or wine. Leave the fruit to stand for at least 30 minutes, stirring occasionally. Just before serving, arrange the fruit decoratively in the meringue baskets.

Angel Cake Casket with Mango Filling

Serves 8

Working time: about 30 minutes

Total time: about 5 hours

Calories 150

Protein 3g

Cholesterol 0mg

Total fat 1g

Saturated fat 0g

Sodium 40mg

5	egg whites	5
$\frac{1}{8}$ tsp	salt	$\frac{1}{8}$ tsp
175 g	caster sugar	6 oz
$\frac{1}{2}$	lemon, finely grated rind only	$\frac{1}{2}$
1 tbsp	fresh lemon juice	1 tbsp
30 g	plain flour	1 oz

30 g	cornflour	1 oz
	icing sugar to decorate	
Mango Filling		
1	mango	1
90 g	fromage frais	3 oz
1½ tsp	gelatine	1½ tsp

Preheat the oven to 180°C (350°F or Mark 4). Lightly grease a 22 by 12 cm (9 by 5 inch) loaf tin. Line its base with greaseproof paper.

Whisk the egg whites with the salt until the whites stand in stiff peaks. Whisk in 125 g (4 oz) of the caster sugar, 1 tablespoon at a time, until the mixture is thick and glossy, then whisk in the lemon rind and juice. Mix the remaining caster sugar with the flours and whisk this in, 1 tablespoon at a time.

Transfer the mixture to the prepared tin and bake it for 35 to 40 minutes until the cake is risen and firm to the touch. Leave it to cool in the tin.

Peel the mango and cut all the flesh away from the stone. Purée the fruit. There should be about 20 cl (7 fl oz). Mix the purée with the *fromage frais*. Sprinkle the gelatine on to 2 tablespoons of

hot water and stand the bowl in a pan of simmering water for about 10 minutes. When the gelatine has absorbed the water, add a little of the fruit mixture to it. Stir the gelatine-fruit mixture into the purée.

Cut down into the cake 2 cm ($\frac{3}{4}$ inch) from the sides to within 2 cm ($\frac{3}{4}$ inch) of the base. Scoop out the centre of the cake with a spoon, to leave a casket with walls and base about 2 cm (3 inch) thick. Pour the mango purée into the casket. Cover the purée with some of the angel cake trimmings to give the cake its original depth. Cover the cake with plastic film and chill it for at least 2 hours.

Loosen edges of cake and invert on to a platter. Dust with icing sugar.

Caraway Seed Sponge

Serves 12

Working time: about 25 minutes

Total time: about 3 hours and 30 minutes

Calories 125

Protein 3g

Cholesterol 60mg

Total fat 3g

Saturated fat 0g

Sodium 70mg

3	eggs separated	3	2 tsp	polyunsaturated margarine	2 tsp
150 g	light brown sugar	5 oz	1 tbsp	orange flower water	1 tbsp
125 g	plain flour	4 oz	1 tsp	caraway seeds	1 tsp
1 tsp	baking powder	1 tsp		icing sugar to decorate	
1½ tbsp	cornflour	1½ tbsp			

Preheat the oven to 200°C (400°F or Mark 6). Grease a 20 cm (8 inch) round cake tin or a petal cake tin approximately 18 cm (7 inches) in diameter. Line the tin with non-stick parchment paper.

Whisk the egg whites until they stand firm in peaks. Gradually whisk in the brown sugar, 1 tablespoon at a time, then quickly fold in the egg yolks. Sift the flour, baking powder and cornflour together two or three times into another bowl, to aerate them very thoroughly. Heat the margarine in a small saucepan until the margarine melts, then remove the pan from the heat and

add the orange flower water and 2 tablespoons of water. Using a metal spoon or a rubber spatula, fold the flour mixture quickly and evenly into the cake mixture, followed by the melted mixture and the caraway seeds. Pour the batter into the prepared tin and bake, until well risen, golden-brown and firm to the touch – 25 to 30 minutes in the round tin, or 30 to 40 minutes in the petal tin.

Turn the cake out on to a wire rack and leave it to cool, then remove the paper. Before serving the cake, sift icing sugar lightly over the top.

Strawberry Cognac Layer Cake

Serves 10

Working time: about 1 hour

Total time: about 10 hours

Calories 175

Protein 8g

Cholesterol 60mg

Total fat 7g

Saturated fat 3g

Sodium 145mg

2	eggs	2
1	egg white	1
90 g	vanilla-flavoured caster sugar	3 oz
90 g	plain flour	3 oz
3 tbsp	cognac	3 tbsp
5 tbsp	skimmed milk	5 tbsp
6 tbsp	whipping cream	6 tbsp

	Strawberry Filling	
250 g	cottage cheese, sieved	8 oz
3 tbsp	skimmed milk	3 tbsp
2 tbsp	clear honey	2 tbsp
1	lemon, grated rind only	1
1 tbsp	fresh lemon juice	1 tbsp
1½ tsp	powdered gelatine	1½ tsp
250 g	strawberries	8 oz

Preheat the oven to 190°C (375°F or Mark 5). Line a loaf tin approx 22 by 11 cm (9 by 4½ inches) and a shallow rectangular tin approximately 32 by 22 cm (13 by 9 inches) with non-stick parchment paper.

Put the eggs, egg white and sugar in a bowl over a pan of simmering water. Whisk until the mixture is very thick and the whisk leaves a heavy trail. Remove mixture from heat and whisk until cool. Sift flour and fold it quickly and evenly into egg mixture. Turn the batter into the shallow tin and level. Cook the sponge for 12 to 15 minutes, until well risen, and firm. Turn on to a wire rack; leave until cold, then peel off the paper.

Beat cottage cheese, milk, honey and lemon rind in a bowl. Put lemon juice in a small bowl and stand it in a pan of gently simmering water. Add gelatine and leave it to dissolve. Stir into cheese mixture. Slice ½ the strawberries and add them to the mixture.

Cut rectangular piece of sponge and set it in the base of the loaf tin. Combine the cognac and the 5 tablespoons of milk and pour 3 tablespoons over the cake in the tin. When the strawberry-cheese mixture thickens, spoon half into the loaf tin. Cut a larger piece of sponge and use it to cover the strawberry-cheese mixture. Soak the sponge with half of the remaining cognac and milk, and spoon in the rest of the strawberry-cheese mix. Cut a final piece of sponge, moisten with cognac and milk and set on top. Refrigerate overnight, then decorate with whipped cream and strawberries.

Dobostorte

Serves 12

Working
time: about
1 hour

Total time:
about
2 hours and
30 minutes

Calories
175

Protein
4g

Cholesterol
65mg

Total fat
5g

Saturated fat
2g

Sodium
35mg

3	eggs	3
125 g	vanilla-flavoured caster sugar	4 oz
125 g	plain flour	4 oz
90 g	granulated sugar	3 oz

30 cl	chocolate-flavoured pastry cream ½ pint
	cream (see page 7)
5 tbsp	whipping cream	5 tbsp
12	hazelnuts, shelled, toasted and	12
	skinned

Preheat oven to 190°C (375°F or Mark 5). Draw two 25 by 11 cm (10 by 4½ inch) rectangles on each of two sheets of parchment paper. Place each, marked side down, on a baking sheet.

Put eggs and vanilla-flavoured sugar in a bowl set over a pan of gently simmering water. Whisk the mixture for about 10 minutes until the eggs are very thick and creamy and the whisk leaves a heavy trail when lifted. Remove bowl from heat and continue whisking until it is cool. Sift the flour and fold it quickly into the egg mixture. Spoon the mixture into the marked rectangles and spread evenly. Cook the sponges for 10 to 12 minutes, until they are firm and a pale golden.

Trim immediately with a serrated knife to fit marks on the paper. Transfer the sponges, still on the paper, to a wire rack to cool.

Select the smoothest sponge for the torte's top layer, but leave it on the paper. Heat granulated sugar in a small heavy-bottomed saucepan, without stirring, until the sugar melts and turns golden. Pour the caramel quickly over the chosen sponge and spread to the edge of the sponge. Before it sets, oil a heavy knife and mark into 12 portions. Leave the caramel to harden.

To assemble, peel one sponge layer off the paper and place it on a dish. Spread the sponge with one third of the chocolate pastry cream. Cover the chocolate layer with a second layer of sponge, more pastry cream, then a third layer of sponge, the remaining chocolate pastry cream and finally the caramel sponge layer. Whip the cream stiffly and spoon it into a piping bag fitted with a large star nozzle. Decorate as illustration, with a hazelnut on each portion.

Yule Log

Serves 12		**Calories** 175
Working time: about 1 hour		**Protein** 2g
		Cholesterol 5mg
Total time: about 2 hours and 30 minutes		**Total fat** 4g
		Saturated fat 2g
		Sodium 25mg

6	egg whites	6
190 g	caster sugar	6½ oz
90 g	plain chocolate, melted and cooled	3 oz
60 g	plain flour, sifted	2 oz
	cocoa powder to decorate	
	icing sugar to decorate	

Chestnut Filling		
200 g	chestnut purée	7 oz
4 tbsp	single cream	4 tbsp
1 tbsp	thick honey	1 tbsp

Preheat the oven to 220°C (425°F or Mark 7). Place a small piece of non-stick parchment paper on a baking sheet. Grease a 32 by 22 cm (13 by 9 inch) Swiss roll tin and line it with parchment paper. Have ready two piping bags fitted with 1.5 cm (½ inch) plain nozzles.

Whisk egg whites in bowl until stiff, then whisk in 175 g (6 oz) of caster sugar, 1 tbsp at a time. For mushrooms decorating, transfer 3 tbsp of the mixture into a smaller bowl, and whisk in 15 g (½ oz) sugar. Spoon the smaller quantity of meringue into a piping bag and pipe stalks and caps on to the parchment paper. Bake on the bottom shelf of the oven.

Return any meringue left in the bag to the bulk of the mixture. Quickly fold in the melted chocolate and the flour. Transfer this mixture to the second piping bag and pipe lines crosswise in the prepared tin. Bake the roulade for about 12 minutes, until risen and just firm. Take it out and switch the oven off, but leave the meringue mushrooms to cool slowly in the oven.

Turn the roulade out on to a sheet of parchment paper and peel off lining paper. Cover the cake with the tin and leave the cake to cool completely.

Beat together the chestnut purée, cream and honey until smooth. Detach the mushrooms from the paper and, using the chestnut filling, attach each stalk to a cap.

Remove the tin and lining paper from the cake and spread it with the filling. Roll up the log starting at a short end using the paper to help. Put on a dish with the mushrooms then dust with cocoa and icing sugar.

Madeleines

Makes 20 madeleines		Calories 65
Working time: about 10 minutes		Protein 1g
		Cholesterol 30mg
Total time: about 35 minutes		Total fat 2g
		Saturated fat 1g
		Sodium 10mg

1	egg	**1**	**90 g**	plain flour	**3 oz**
1	egg white	**1**	**45 g**	unsalted butter, melted and cooled	**1½ oz**
90 g	caster sugar	**3 oz**			
1 tbsp	amaretto liqueur	**1 tbsp**	**1 tbsp**	vanilla sugar	**1 tbsp**

Preheat the oven to 200°C (400°F or Mark 6). Butter twenty 7.5 cm (3 inch) madeleine moulds and dust them lightly with flour.

Put the egg and egg white into a bowl with the caster sugar and amaretto. Whisk the mixture until it thickens to the consistency of unwhipped double cream. Sift the flour lightly over the surface of the mixture, then fold it in very carefully with a metal spoon or rubber spatula.

Gently fold in the melted butter.

Half fill each madeleine mould with mixture. Bake the madeleines for 15 to 20 minutes, until well risen, lightly browned and springy to to the touch. Carefully turn them out of the moulds on to a wire rack and immediately sift the vanilla sugar over them. Serve the madeleines while still warm, or allow them to cool.

Raspberry-Filled Shells

Makes		
18 shells		
Working		
time: about		
40 minutes		
Total time:		
about		
1 hour and		
40 minutes		

Calories	
107	
Protein	
2g	
Cholesterol	
50mg	
Total fat	
6g	
Saturated fat	
3g	
Sodium	
20mg	

3	eggs	**3**
90 g	caster sugar	**3 oz**
90 g	plain flour	**3 oz**
¼ litre	whipping cream, whipped	**8 fl oz**

350 g	fresh raspberries, or frozen	**12 oz**
	raspberries, thawed	
1 tbsp	icing sugar	**1 tbsp**

Preheat the oven to 180°C (350°F or Mark 4). Grease 18 rounded, shell-patterned bun moulds and dust the moulds lightly with flour.

To make the sponge, put the eggs and caster sugar in a large bowl. Place the bowl over a saucepan of hot, but not boiling, water on a low heat. Whisk until the mixture becomes thick and very pale in colour. Remove the bowl from the heat and continue whisking until the mixture is cool and will hold a ribbon trail almost indefinitely. Sift the flour very lightly over the top of the whisked mixture and fold it in carefully with a large metal spoon or a rubber spatula.

Divide the sponge batter equally among the 18 bun moulds and spread it evenly. Bake the sponges for 25 to 30 minutes until very well risen, lightly browned and springy to the touch. Turn the sponges out of the moulds on to a wire rack to cool, rounded sides up.

Cut each sponge in half, at a slight angle to the horizontal. Cover the bottom halves with cream and raspberries and set the top halves on the filling at an angle, so that the cakes resemble half-open clams. Sift the icing sugar over the cakes.

Useful weights and measures

Weight Equivalents

Avoirdupois		Metric
1 ounce	=	28.35 grams
1 pound	=	254.6 grams
2.3 pounds	=	1 kilogram

Liquid Measurements

$^1/_4$ pint	=	$1^1/_2$ decilitres
$^1/_2$ pint	=	$^1/_4$ litre
scant 1 pint	=	$^1/_2$ litre
$1^3/_4$ pints	=	1 litre
1 gallon	=	4.5 litres

Liquid Measures

1 pint	= 20 fl oz	= 32 tablespoons
$^1/_2$ pint	= 10 fl oz	= 16 tablespoons
$^1/_4$ pint	= 5 fl oz	= 8 tablespoons
$^1/_8$ pint	= $2^1/_2$ fl oz	= 4 tablespoons
$^1/_{16}$ pint	= $1^1/_4$ fl oz	= 2 tablespoons

Solid Measures

1 oz almonds, ground = $3^3/_4$ level tablespoons

1 oz breadcrumbs fresh = 7 level tablespoons

1 oz butter, lard = 2 level tablespoons

1 oz cheese, grated = $3^1/_2$ level tablespoons

1 oz cocoa = $2^3/_4$ level tablespoons

1 oz desiccated coconut = $4^1/_2$ tablespoons

1 oz cornflour = $2^1/_2$ tablespoons

1 oz custard powder = $2^1/_2$ tablespoons

1 oz curry powder and spices = 5 tablespoons

1 oz flour = 2 level tablespoons

1 oz rice, uncooked = $1^1/_2$ tablespoons

1 oz sugar, caster and granulated = 2 tablespoons

1 oz icing sugar = $2^1/_2$ tablespoons

1 oz yeast, granulated = 1 level tablespoon

American Measures

16 fl oz	=1 American pint
8 fl oz	=1 American standard cup
0.50 fl oz	=1 American tablespoon

(*slightly smaller than British Standards Institute tablespoon*)

0.16 fl oz	=1 American teaspoon

Australian Cup Measures

(*Using the 8-liquid-ounce cup measure*)

1 cup flour	4 oz
1 cup sugar (crystal or caster)	8 oz
1 cup icing sugar (free from lumps)	5 oz
1 cup shortening (butter, margarine)	8 oz
1 cup brown sugar (lightly packed)	4 oz
1 cup soft breadcrumbs	2 oz
1 cup dry breadcrumbs	3 oz
1 cup rice (uncooked)	6 oz
1 cup rice (cooked)	5 oz
1 cup mixed fruit	4 oz
1 cup grated cheese	4 oz
1 cup nuts (chopped)	4 oz
1 cup coconut	$2^1/_2$ oz

Australian Spoon Measures

	level tablespoon
1 oz flour	2
1 oz sugar	$1^1/_2$
1 oz icing sugar	2
1 oz shortening	1
1 oz honey	1
1 oz gelatine	2
1 oz cocoa	3
1 oz cornflour	$2^1/_2$
1 oz custard powder	$2^1/_2$

Australian Liquid Measures

(*Using 8-liquid-ounce cup*)

1 cup liquid	8 oz
$2^1/_2$ cups liquid	20 oz (1 pint)
2 tablespoons liquid	1 oz
1 gill liquid	5 oz ($^1/_4$ pint)